"Kimber Simpkins is an auth[e]  planet, and this book is her tor generation of women committe[d] and secrecy around our relations ings. This book resonated with [me ... as a] woman and a spiritual practitioner. I highly recommend Kimber's book for any woman who is ready to let down the burden of food and self-esteem issues. It has the potential to act as a catalytic force toward healing, and ultimately to living a more authentic life."

—**Katie Silcox**, author of the New York Times bestseller
Healthy Happy Sexy

"Kimber Simpkins's inspiring journey to finding peace with food and her body lays an amazing groundwork for *52 Ways to Love Your Body*, and her insights and suggestions within this book are powerful and practical to implement. So many of us know the body image struggle all too well, and I'm so glad Kimber shines a bright light of hope and inspiration in her work!"

—**Dina Proctor**, author of *Madly Chasing Peace*

"What a powerful, practical, and heartfelt handbook on how to shift the inner conversation to compassion. Kimber speaks to us in the most supportive guiding voice—that of a trusted friend, which to me is a true love guru."

—**Melanie Salvatore-August**, author of *Kitchen Yoga*

"Think it's impossible to love your body? Think again! The compassion and wisdom Kimber brings to her fifty-two strategies is sure to convince you to end the war with your body and, instead, treat it the way you would a best friend. This gem of a book is going straight to my waiting room, and I hope all of my clients will read it."

—**Judith Matz, LCSW**, coauthor of *The Diet Survivor's Handbook* and *Beyond a Shadow of a Diet*, and author of *Amanda's Big Dream*

"*52 Ways to Love Your Body* offers dozens of powerful exercises to help you love the skin you're in, and live a happier, fuller life as a result. Try even a handful of Kimber's suggestions and you'll likely feel a lot better about what you see in the mirror— and about yourself."

—**Lori Deschene**, founder of www.tinybuddha.com, and author of *Tiny Buddha's 365 Tiny Love Challenges*

"*52 Ways to Love Your Body* outlines the path to sustaining body acceptance. Kimber brings in just the right amounts of spirituality, wisdom, and compassion to the timely topic of weight. This book will help individuals ditch the diet culture for good."

—**Signe Darpinian, MFT**, author of *Knock Out Dieting*

"Only once in a while do I pick up a book that speaks truths to me on so many levels. I've been involved in social work and the body acceptance movement for years, and there is a reoccurring challenge we face above all else: the want to love and treasure your own body exists, but the knowledge on how to go about it isn't as easily grasped. Kimber fills this need for practical ways to learn that love with *52 Ways to Love Your Body*. Throughout the book, she furnishes the reader with positive ways to embrace ourselves just as we are, and exercises to strengthen that appreciation for our friend, our body. I firmly believe this book will redefine how readers approach their relationships with their bodies, and what it means to nurture themselves. I've already recommended it to a client and it isn't available yet—that's how strongly I feel about this book. It's a resource for all women like myself, those of us learning to love ourselves in a world telling us we have no reason to; this book is a calm voice of reason reminding us of all the reasons we should."

—**Kai Hibbard**, body acceptance activist, writer, and weight loss reality TV survivor

"*52 Ways to Love Your Body* offers an excellent step-by-step guide to inspire and support readers in the process of cultivating and nurturing love for the bodies they're in right now."

—**Melanie Klein**, professor of sociology and women's studies, and coeditor of *Yoga and Body Image*

52 Ways to love your body

KIMBER SIMPKINS

New Harbinger Publications, Inc.

Publisher's Note

This publication is designed to provide accurate and authoritative information in regard to the subject matter covered. It is sold with the understanding that the publisher is not engaged in rendering psychological, financial, legal, or other professional services. If expert assistance or counseling is needed, the services of a competent professional should be sought.

Distributed in Canada by Raincoast Books

Copyright © 2016 by Kimber Simpkins
New Harbinger Publications, Inc.
5674 Shattuck Avenue
Oakland, CA 94609
www.newharbinger.com

Cover design by Debbie Berne
Acquired by Catharine Meyers
Edited by Rona Bernstein

Library of Congress Cataloging-in-Publication Data

Simpkins, Kimber, author.
  Fifty-two ways to love your body / Kimber Simpkins.
      pages cm
  Includes bibliographical references.
  ISBN 978-1-62625-379-7 (pbk. : alk. paper) -- ISBN 978-1-62625-380-3 (pdf e-book) -- ISBN 978-1-62625-381-0 (epub) 1. Body image in women. 2. Self-acceptance in women. I. Title. II. Title: 52 ways to love your body.
  BF697.5.B63S555 2015
  306.4'613--dc23

                            2015032694

Printed in the United States of America

18   17   16

10   9   8   7   6   5   4   3   2   1   First printing

Contents

Introduction

S tanding at my locker one day in middle school, a friend shoved a torn advertisement into my hand. "It's Laura," she said. "Look. She's a model for Mallstroms." The black and white newsprint photos showed a fresh-faced Laura, a girl one grade above us, frolicking in a series of perfectly fitted string bikinis. "Don't you hate her?" my friend whispered. My mouth dropped open, but nothing came out. She pulled the scrap loose from my fingers and turned to another friend to commiserate.

Shoving my books around the locker's messy shelf, my mind whirled. I didn't hate Laura. I hated *myself*. Why did Laura get to be a model and not me? What was desirable about her body and hopelessly flawed about mine? Clearly I was wrong…and she was right.

Shame crept up my neck and over my cheekbones. I wasn't good enough, wasn't pretty enough, wasn't enough, period. The urge flooded me to empty my locker of books and climb inside it to hide for the rest of the day, but I was too big to fit between the metal walls. Laura could probably hide in her locker, but why would she? She was a freaking model!

Worst of all, I had no one to tell. There was not a single person in the world I trusted to hear not only the shame I felt about my body, but also the added layer of self-disgust over hating my body to begin with, and the fact that I would have gladly gift-wrapped my soul to be in Laura's place. My only consolation was the thought, *Just one more hour until lunch. It's mac and cheese day. And a bake sale later. Maybe they'll have mint brownies.*

I carried shame and its ravenous pal, insatiable hunger, well past middle school, into two careers and motherhood, until I finally decided my life didn't have room for them anymore: that story I told in *Full: How I Learned to Satisfy My Insatiable Hunger and Feed My Soul*.[1] Today, as a yoga teacher and body love explorer, I teach women how to love their bodies.

Some of you have already looked at the photo on the book cover and thought, *Oh, that's easy for her to say. Look at her body. She's not living in my body; she doesn't know how hard it is.*

Well, that's true. I don't know what it's like to live in your body. What I do know is that I spent twenty-five years hating my body, the same body you see in that photo. It was painful and so lonely. I wish more than anything that I could take back every second and every bit of energy I wasted thinking my body wasn't worth loving.

Let's see, if I count up all the seconds, minutes, and hours I spent grieving over my stretch marks, counting the calories of tasteless food, and cursing the gods for not giving me the naturally thin, high-metabolism, mannequin-esque body I desperately wanted—if I could get all that time back—maybe I could have written ten more life-altering books, cured cancer, and saved a small island nation from climate change, or at least given it all a good shot.

So with all that in mind, let me ask you this: Do you think that every second you spend disliking your body is any better spent than the time I spent disliking mine? What would you do if you could have all that time back?

Learning to love your body means no longer wasting your energy on body hatred and giving yourself back all that time to change the world instead. The book you're holding in your hands, *52 Ways to Love Your Body*, will help you on that path. On these pages I share with you many of my favorite ways to treat my body with love and let go of the yearning for perfection, feed my true hungers, and free myself of the mean girl voice I bullied myself with for years. And best of all, these practices not only have helped me, but also have been life changing for the many students in my workshops whose shift from body hating to body loving I've been lucky enough to witness.

I know it may feel impossible to believe that you could make peace with your body and even learn to love it. Maybe you've spent your entire life until now wishing your body were different, and you're thinking that one little book isn't going to change that. But change is based on practice, and you have to begin somewhere. That's what I'm offering you—practices that can change your life.

Enjoy the inspiration and practices in whatever way works best for you, whether it's by opening up the book and dropping into a chapter that sounds enticing, or feasting on it all the way through, or savoring a single exercise at a time. You probably noticed that there are fifty-two exercises, and fifty-two weeks in a year, which is not a coincidence: you can relish one chapter each week over the course of the year to give yourself a full year of self-guided body love. Let the practices here inspire and support your quest to become the friend your body deserves. By coming this far, you're already on your way.

1

You CAN Change

A friend once said to me, "You can't just change how you feel about your body. You can try to diet and look better and maybe you'll like your body more then. But you can't just up and decide to love your body when you don't see anything worth loving."

Her words are the perfect summation of where so many of us start this journey; it's where I began. Changing how I felt about my body meant that I would love it as soon as my thighs fit into my favorite jeans from seven years ago, as soon as my body cooperated with the rigorous daily gym routine I'd planned for it (preferably by going without me), as soon as my belly felt full all the time without a single drop of cellulite visible on or around it. My love was withheld until some magic day when, having achieved perfection, my body would deserve better than a constant stream of nit-picking pinches.

One overcast afternoon, while I was sitting on a park bench and watching a group of children play, it occurred to me—that day was never going to come. Never. For years my body and I had been locked in an endless struggle of dieting and bingeing, forced exercise, and feeling hungry all the time. Something about the way the dim light shadowed the pavement reminded me of the cold winter in high school I spent starving myself to some mythical state of happy thinness. Those chilly days when my body had shrunk to its tiniest did not bring the elation and self-satisfaction I'd hoped for. Instead, isolated from my friends (it's amazing how friendships grow over shared candy and cans of soda) and wearing baggy clothes to hide my deadly experiment, I fought to ignore the empty ache in my stomach that had somehow seeped into my bones and pores: misery was eating me alive.

Shivering under the gray sky, recalling those desolate days, I realized that thinness wouldn't make me happy. I'd already tried that. If my mind was unhappy with my body no matter what size it was, maybe the problem wasn't my body. I needed to teach my mind to be happy with what it's got.

If that sounds kind of scary to you—if you're thinking, *I'm not sure I want to be happy with what I've got*—I hear you. I wasn't sure either. You don't have to be sure. Let whatever longing that led you to pick up this book take your hand and lead you in the direction of more kindness toward yourself, whatever inner and outer hurdles you might have to leap over. You've got this. In the words of Rainer Maria Rilke, "Just keep going."[2]

Here's the good news: our minds are more flexible than we think. Ongoing research by neuroscientists and psychologists like Rick Hanson, author of *Buddha's Brain*, shows that we can change how our minds work by shifting our thoughts in the direction we want them to go. Not once, not twice, but over and over. With time and patience, our patterns of thinking and acting shift to reflect what we really want for ourselves: genuine happiness instead of merely the outer appearance of it.[3]

You can change how you feel about your body. It doesn't happen overnight, but rather with little, repeated nudges. A big container ship that departs from San Francisco makes very slight adjustments in its navigation initially to end up eventually in Tokyo—or Sydney. Those seemingly tiny shifts add up to big changes in the long run.

When have you changed the way you feel about someone or something in your life? Did the change happen when you received more information or when you had a watershed experience? Did things change because of some epiphany or by creating a new routine? How did your beliefs about yourself shift as a result? How did your life benefit? Many years ago I started doing yoga for just twenty minutes a day several times a week and found that my body soon felt stronger and more at ease in the world. Have you had an experience like this? Pause and notice how you've already changed a belief or pattern in your life. Remind yourself that change is something you are capable of, even good at.

Imagine how it would feel to change the way you see yourself. What would it be like to quiet the negative voices and teach your mind to speak to you with encouragement and friendliness? Let yourself sense how much more emotional energy you would have to meet both the obstacles and awesomeness of life. Begin to imagine what you'll do with all that extra energy and time you will have freed up. What would be possible in your life?

2

Get Curious

I have a big colorful reminder written on the wall of my bedroom. It says, "Be curious." My friend Marissa loves being curious—she says embracing curiosity was like finding the magic key to open her heart to more kindness. When she finds herself becoming judgmental, she gets curious instead. For years she'd wanted to declutter her apartment but found that standard advice like "Just get a box and put ten things in it" pressed her inner panic button. *But what if I need this candleholder? What if I regret that I don't have it later? Why is this so hard for me? Everyone else seems to get rid of stuff just fine.* When she grew curious—instead of judgmental—about why she wanted to keep this candleholder or that jewelry box, she could see that she didn't entirely trust that if she needed a jewelry box sometime in the future, she would find another one. "By being curious, I realized it wasn't just about things, but about being able to trust that I could take care of my needs. Curiosity let me be kinder to myself with more honesty and humor. I could see what was funny about holding onto a jewelry box without any jewelry in it."

Try exploring your curiosity right now. What are your hands doing? Feel how they're holding this book. Notice if they feel heavy or light, strong or weak, hard or soft, tingly or numb, cold or warm. Can you notice the sensations in your hands without judging them or trying to fix them? Just observe your hands with friendly interest. What are they up to? Notice how your hands feel, and then get curious about how your mind reacts to them. Does your mind want to change or shift something, do something different? Maybe it comes up with a task for you, such as, *I need to use more moisturizer*, or *Right, schedule manicure*. Maybe even a judgment comes up like, *What's wrong with me that I can't even take care of my hands?* If so, notice how easily, with a small shift in your attention, your mind generates a to-do list or criticism. Your job here is to notice that, too, and be curious about how your mind works.

Get curious doesn't mean get analytical and examine yourself like an algae sample squashed between slides under a microscope. We have a tendency to get hard and even mean when we look at ourselves too closely. Curiosity invites us to be more childlike; more willing to see the big picture as well as the details; more interested, inquisitive, and at times awestruck. We don't have to fix anything, we just look. Get curious about your thoughts, your feelings, why you reached for your cup of tea at just that moment, why you chose the blue yogurt to go in your cart rather than the red one. See if you can notice without judgment. Meet each action with a little smile on your face and a friendly tilt of the head. Don't even try to figure yourself out yet. Just let yourself notice everything with curiosity.

Curiosity is powerful and friendly. Let yours be soft and open, with a willingness to see and take in everything about yourself without judgment. To practice, pick one activity today to get curious about, whether it's folding laundry, driving to work, eating a snack, or walking the dog. It's easier to practice being curious alone, but if it's hard to find time alone, practice it wherever and whenever you can, using the following as a guide:

1. Wherever you plan to practice, feel your feet on the ground and take one or two deep breaths.

2. Set your intention to be curious without judgment.

3. Do your activity, and watch yourself doing it.

4. Notice the feelings and sensations that arise.

5. Be curious about how your mind reacts to the activity.

6. If you notice yourself judging, be curious about that, too! Then keep observing.

7. Give yourself credit for whatever level of curiosity you were able to bring to the situation.

Try to get curious as often as you can during your day, no matter what you're doing or what thoughts, feelings, or sensations arise. Wear a special piece of jewelry or string around your wrist to remind you to get curious throughout your day. Let curiosity be your magic key for allowing your mind and body to work together to love yourself as you are.

3

Just Say Hi

When I first heard about affirmations, I thought, *Well, that would be awesome. All I have to do is look in the mirror and say, "Hey Kimber, you're beautiful. And I love you!" and all my terrible body-hating problems will go away. How great would that be?* I skipped over and peered into the bathroom mirror, and before even taking a first breath and trying to repeat the magical sentence to myself, the usual chorus of awful criticism started singing their complaints: "Your face is as round as a pie!" the bass line hummed. "All those wrinkles and pimples make you sad," the mid-range voices chimed in as the soprano sang in a high-pitched tone, "I can't stand to look at yoooooooooou!"

I couldn't mumble a single affirmation over the ruckus. I needed to turn the volume down on the complaint choir before even considering saying something kind to myself in the mirror. Silence would be a nice start. Could I look in the mirror and not say anything at all? Maybe just a hello? Maybe I could offer myself the same basic level of friendliness I would offer a friendly stranger. "Hey there, how are you? How's your day?" I would never go up to a stranger and start ranting at her about how I hate her hair, and her eyes are the wrong color, and why does she persist in wearing that ugly shirt? We deserve at least as much consideration as we would give someone we barely know—and possibly a lot more.

Elizabeth Gilbert tells a story about how she once walked into a hotel elevator and saw a familiar face approaching her that she sort of recognized, but couldn't place. She laughed when she realized she'd eagerly rushed toward a reflection of herself, thinking she was greeting a friend she hadn't seen in a long time. She wrote to herself, "Never forget that once upon a time, in an unguarded moment, you recognized yourself as a friend."[4]

Looking into the mirror without giving yourself a hard time is the first step in this direction. Can you look in the mirror without criticizing yourself? Just look in the mirror and say hi, like greeting a friendly stranger? No judgment, just hello.

Here's how:

1. Start out by setting your intention to not judge yourself.

2. Stand close to a mirror without looking into it.

3. Take a few deep breaths.

4. Peek in the mirror and see if you can just say hi to yourself.

Notice if it's hard to do. Notice if it makes you teary or frustrated. You can always stop and try again later. Notice if trying makes you laugh. Play peek-a-boo with the mirror a little bit; make it playful and fun if you can. When I first started this practice, I could look in the mirror for about a nanosecond before my critical voices went operatic. Give yourself credit for whatever tiny length of time you're able to look in the mirror without criticizing. Try to increase the amount of time to longer periods, a breath or two or ten. Then try it whenever you catch your reflection during the day, when passing windows and mirrors, wherever you are. Just say hi.

4

The Black Box

All the incidents and feelings that make up our body image and impact our hunger get saved in the "black box" of our minds, tucked away where we can't see or hear the clicks and whirrings. Not only do we often avoid telling anyone how the yelled insult (or compliment) affected us, but many times we aren't even aware of it ourselves.

I never told anyone how the girls at sleepaway camp made fun of my "fat" calves for the entire week while we swam and changed and slept in the same cabin together. I told no one, not a single friend, how hunger consumed my thoughts; how even after eating an entire two-scoop ice cream cone with my favorite flavors—mint chocolate chip and caramel fudge—I could still eat more. Much more.

The black box is a hidden repository of those very things we are most ashamed of, those crisis moments that never get discussed unless we've been lucky enough to end up on the couch of a loving friend or therapist. We feel ashamed of our bodies and our hunger, we feel ashamed of our shame, then we pack it all in this shadowy corner of our minds and try desperately to pretend it doesn't exist.

As an adult, I hid how much I disliked my legs, wrapping my disgust tightly in duct tape and hiding it in some deserted nook of my brain. When I overheard another woman across a café complaining about her fat thighs and how she was going to have to lose a million pounds to fit into her favorite jeans, I found myself so triggered that my brain could no longer keep track of my friend's story about her dying grandmother. My eyes took in my friend's teary cheeks, but my mind was far away, thinking how if that woman's thighs were big, then mine must be huge, and if she needed to lose a million pounds, I must need to lose a trillion. This self-obsessed-bad-friend scenario played out more often than I'd like to admit.

At some point, I grew tired of forcibly restraining my thoughts and realized I needed to open the black box and let some air and sunlight inside. In order to work honestly with how we feel about our bodies, we need the courage to look at the unexamined beliefs, the triggers, and the tender wounded places, and ask them what they need in order to heal. You've got to open the black box. You've got to be brave enough to tell the stories you've never told and admit to the pain you've never let yourself feel fully.

It's a big deal to admit, even to ourselves, that we have stories like these about our bodies. But it can be even harder to carry those stories without ever sharing them. Find a compassionate listener—a trusted friend, partner, family member, or therapist—to share them with. Having your story witnessed by someone who cares about you is healing in and of itself. Hearing that person's story of vulnerability can let you know that you're not alone, and you never have been.

And once you've done it, remind yourself of how courageous it is to open and to share, how much honesty and love it takes to see yourself clearly.

Some ways to open the black box:

1. Journal your stories of shame about your body and hunger. Start with prompts such as, "I've never told anyone this, but one time…," "My most embarrassing moment with my body was when…," "The first time I remember feeling shame about my body…"

2. Find a friend who would be (a) willing to hear your story and (b) hopefully willing to share his or her own.

3. If you can't find a friend, you may decide to post your story anonymously in a safe online "love your body" community space. Be cautious about this: find one that is carefully monitored and doesn't allow trolling (i.e., posting inflammatory comments), such as https://www.facebook.com/groups/howtoloveyourbody.

4. Reach out to a therapist or support group in your area to share your story with a professional and hear others' stories about struggling with body image and hunger.

5

Give Yourself Permission

M ore than once, I've had a woman come up to me, take a deep breath, and express some version of the following: "I'm tired of being told I should love my body. It's fine and dandy for people like you—I know you don't think so, but it's true—with bodies like yours. But what about those of us whose bodies just aren't lovable? No one could love my body, and no number of idiotic affirmations on repeat will ever change that. Maybe if I got some plastic surgery, maybe if I lost sixty pounds, maybe if I could quit my job and work out all day instead, maybe if I hadn't had three pregnancies—one with twins—then I could have a body worth loving." She usually stops and takes another deep breath: "I hate my body. Trying to love it feels pointless and stupid and I don't know what to do about it."

Normally I can't give the woman in front of me the response this painful confession merits, but I'll try to offer some love here.

You are in such a hard place. I've been stuck there, or some dark spot like it. It's like the smoking rooms you sometimes still see at the airport—let's call it the Unworthy Room—and when you're locked behind its glass, you feel all alone in the world, trapped and doomed. You stand touching the glass wall, your fingertips making delicate smears on the window surface, wishing you could be on the outside, but it's impossible. For years I stood in that room, watching all the shiny, happy people walk by, holding hands, celebrating their successes, doing things I wanted to do but couldn't because I was too dumb, too heavy, and too ugly.

But every once in a while, I saw someone shuffle by who looked like me, uncertain, insecure, stumbling a little, and then I watched her pick herself up, dust off her chalky knees, and keep going. *She's doing it*, I thought. *She doesn't care if she's disheveled and lost.* Later I would see her again, this time walking with her head a little higher, shoulders back, tripping a moment on a wayward edge of carpet, then straightening up and moving on.

Watching my person inspired me to stand back a little bit and look at the room I'd been living in for so long. How did I end up here? Why can't I leave? I'd heard the messages all my life: you're not good enough, you don't belong, you're all wrong. Those voices built the room for me. And then I walked into it and stayed there for one simple reason: I believed them. And the reason I couldn't find the door to leave? It wasn't because the door was locked or someone else had the key. It was because I was waiting for someone outside the door to let me out, to tell me I was worthy and that I was invited to join the world. I was waiting for permission to leave.

Sociologist Brené Brown says that the difference between people who believe they are worthy of love and belonging and the people who don't is that the first group believes that they are worthy of love and belonging.[5] That's all. You are worthy if you believe it. Losing (or gaining) weight doesn't make us worthy. The absence or presence of stretch marks on our legs, butts, and arms doesn't determine our worthiness. That kid who yelled "Ugly" at you when you caught his ball on the playground? He also doesn't get to weigh in on the question of your worthiness. Only one person does.

You don't need permission to leave the Unworthy Room. Or rather, the only permission you need is your own. Give yourself permission to leave. This is your first step: trust that you are not alone. Look for people who inspire you, whom you recognize as being like you—all those messed up, not-okay folks walking around outside of the Unworthy Room. They are out there. Find them. (Here's a little secret: everyone has an Unworthy Room. You'd be surprised by how many people walking around out there feel vulnerable and not okay. I'm one of them.)

Next, tell the walls of the Unworthy Room that you have an important appointment with the rest of your life. Turn your back on whoever fed you the belief that your bulges and bumps aren't worthy of love no matter what they look like, just because they're yours. Walk out on whoever imposed on us the expectation that flawless bodies are the only ones worthy of love, instead of reminding us that bodies with rolls and pain and scars are beautiful and lovable just the way they are. As you swing the door open wide, announce to the world that your worthiness is not negotiable, your body is valuable in every cell and square inch of flesh, and you are not withholding love from yourself anymore.

Then let yourself feel smart and victorious and grateful for a while. Go get some dinner. You are worthy. You rescued yourself. You walked out the door. Go and do your thing.

Some days (or nights, as is usually the case for me) you'll find yourself in the Unworthy Room again, despite all your efforts. Let yourself take a rest behind the glass, remembering how long you lived here. Then when you're ready, locate your inspiration and brush off your knees. Give up on the room instead of on yourself. Give yourself permission to walk out the door and into Life as many times as it takes, until you forget where the Unworthy Room is altogether, until you know beyond any reasonable doubt that your worthiness does not decrease with age or cellulite or stretch marks, or with other people's judgments about your worthiness and value. It doesn't even depend on your own. Go, dear, go.

6

Be Your Own Best Friend

When my son Cooper was little, he loved to ice skate with his friend Emily at the local skating rink. It was fun to watch the two of them skate and tumble around the rink in their puffy coats and mittens. One afternoon while I was picking up Cooper from preschool, Emily's dad said to me, "I've got to tell you what Emily told me last night after we got home from skating: 'My body is my best friend.'" Emily's words struck my heart like a bell that even now reverberates through my life. I had always thought of my body more as an enemy or a stranger. I wondered, *What if I treated my body like my best friend?*

Pretty much everything would have to change about how I treated my body to start to think of it as my best friend. First, if my body were my best friend, I wouldn't nitpick at her and give her a hard time for her appearance. I certainly wouldn't walk up to her and say, "You look like crap! What were you thinking when you put on those pants this morning?" In fact, if someone said something like that to my best friend, I'd tell the offender to back off and leave her alone, and then I'd take my friend aside, tell her what an idiot that person was, and take her out for a hike or a yoga class or anything to help her to remember how wonderful she is.

When my best friend is tired, I don't berate her for being lazy. I tell her to take a nap, put her feet up, and reschedule our hike. When she's injured or sick, I don't go off on a long rant about how it's all her fault and scold, "Look what you've done to yourself, tsk, tsk." Instead, I offer to bring her soup and sit with her on the couch to binge-watch silly TV shows until she starts to feel better. We're best friends even when things aren't going well, maybe especially when life is giving us nothing but rocks, potholes, and parking tickets. Why not treat our bodies this way too?

Relating to my body like a best friend changed everything. For so long, I had allowed my mind to act like a loud, uber-critical, super-bossy perfectionist with an empathy deficiency and to treat my body as if it were an intentionally disobedient dog with hygiene issues. My mind had to shift to seeing my body as an equal, a peer, a wise being with needs and longings and a tender language all its own. I had to learn to get quiet and listen to it, take it seriously, and respond to it with soft attention.

Friendships have ups and downs—even best friends have painful misunderstandings. Sometimes I get mad at my body, and sometimes my body gets annoyed with me, especially when we haven't moved off the couch in a long time, or when we've been sitting too long in front of the computer. When I've sniped at my body or lobbed a wildly inappropriate comparison at it, I apologize, and we go on. When my body is exhausted or injured, I can tell it's saying to me, "I'm so sorry. I wanted to go on a big adventure, too. Can we reschedule?"

Pause and think about how you treat your best friend. What do you say to her and how do you say it? What kinds of things do you do with your best friend? What do you do when your friend is feeling sad and upset? What do you do when she's having a fantastic day? Contemplate for a moment, then read and finish the sentences below for yourself:

If I really believed my body was my best friend, I would treat myself…

If I really believed my body was my best friend, I would never…

If I really believed my body was my best friend, I would always…

If I really believed my body was my best friend, I would try to…

Finally, what's stopping you from being your body's best friend?

When you find yourself giving your body a hard time, ask yourself, *How would I treat my body if it were my best friend?* And do whatever that friendly thing is.

7

Soothe Yourself

When you get triggered or upset, how do you respond? A trigger can be anything—remembering something you forgot to do, hearing about a friend's diagnosis, overhearing a comment around the water cooler—anything that distresses you and sets your mind spinning. Many of us find it difficult to calm and reassure ourselves, or self-soothe, when we make a mistake or feel hurt, stressed, or angry. When we can soothe ourselves in the moment, we can be more constructive and effective in dealing with whatever life is asking us to handle. Otherwise, many of us end up taking out our hidden agitation on the body and start blaming it for whatever is going wrong. Comforting ourselves is a great way to avoid treating the body as a scapegoat.

When our big family dog got upset about the strong wind rattling the house recently, we let him crawl up onto our laps on the couch, hugged him and stroked his furry head, and told him that we loved him until he felt reassured enough to leap down and meet the scary sounds on his own again. But so often when we're upset, we forget that there's a being inside us who needs to be held, cuddled, and loved.

How often during the day are you triggered by something someone says about dieting or food, or by an unfortunate glance in the mirror that you feel indisputably proves you don't have a best side? It can be something as simple as a weight-loss ad that pops up on your screen while you're answering a work email, and pow! You end up spending the rest of the day's hours managing how triggered you are…unable to focus or calm yourself down.

A single unattractive photo (taken of my butt during a game of Twister) once sent me into a week-long diatribe about how ugly I was. Nowadays, when I see myself about to be derailed by the inner critic's rant, I self-soothe. I notice I'm upset, take a few deep breaths, and let myself feel the intensity of the trigger for a moment. Then I place a hand over my heart and repeat to myself the words that soften my ruffled feathers: "We're in this together, sweetie. We're gonna be okay."

What if you could step out of that spiral before it knocks you over? Use this practice to offer yourself a moment of reassurance, comfort, and relief. Let it help you get on with your day and your life.

Steps to self-soothe:

1. Know what you find soothing. What words or practices are able to help you relax and soften toward yourself and the situation? Staying with the breath, making a cup of tea, placing your hand over your heart, wrapping yourself up in a blanket, repeating the words of a poem, listening to music, going for a walk, interrupting negative self-talk, and offering yourself words that are positive and friendly are just a few examples. "It's going to be okay," "This isn't going to last," "I'm doing the best I can..." Find words that resonate with you. Make a list of self-soothing practices that don't involve food or alcohol.

2. Know that you're triggered. Be familiar with the signs that you are upset, sad, or agitated, and acknowledge your feelings without judgment. Try saying to yourself, "I'm feeling angry," without getting too caught up in why. Even notice where the feeling is in your body.

3. Offer yourself one of your self-soothing practices. Repeat as often as needed.

8

What's Love Got to Do with It?

W hat does "love your body" mean? It doesn't mean that you fall passionately in love with your body, or that you never have another "I hate my body" moment. If we're in a relationship with the body, we're more likely to love it the way we love a sibling or a close friend, which means days when we can't imagine life without them and days when we want to permanently block their number on the phone.

The ancient Greeks had words for love the way we have tea selections or café coffee menus. They expected life to include passionate love, playful love, the love you have for a dear friend, love that grows over a long period of time, and even self-love.[6] Passionate love, or Eros, is how we think of love nowadays, but if you never expect to feel romantic love for your body...me neither. Yet all those other kinds of love are totally doable! That's a lot of love!

Love in its many guises flows when I dance with my hula hoops bouncing around my hips, when I go outside and lie on a quilt in the grass, when I touch my belly and remember everything my body and I have been through together, and when I think about all the ways my body shows up for me every day, whether I say thanks or not. We can cultivate the same feelings of love and intimacy we have with others with our bodies, too.

Which of these feelings and experiences do you have in your relationships?

Affection	Connection	Forgiveness
Goofiness	Listening	Kindness
Fun	Feeling heard	Feeling understood
Enjoyment	Honesty	
Reassurance	Irritation	Humor
Comfort	Misunderstanding	Steadiness
Pleasure	Hurt	Ability to be yourself

We don't experience all of these all the time. Notice when you experience them in relationship with your body and when you don't.

We build relationships based on the time we spend together and what we have in common. In a relationship, it's good to know what the other person enjoys. Do you know what your body likes to do? What are three things you know make your body happy (for example, massages, fun movement, fresh food, time spent in water)? Be specific. Feel free to close your eyes and ask your body directly. Then find out what things your body doesn't enjoy. What makes it irritable and mad at you?

Just as in a friendship, to nurture a better relationship with your body, generously give it what it enjoys and refrain from what it hates as often as possible. See if your relationship grows.

9

Touch Your Breath

Y ou take about 20,000 breaths every day.[7] But most of us barely notice, even though without the breath our lives would shorten to mere minutes. It's one of those things we only notice when it's hard to breathe, when we have an asthma attack, or hyperventilate, or get jabbed hard by a running elbow that knocks the wind out of us. In those moments of crisis we realize how much we need the breath and everything it does for us. The breath acts like a steadily swinging pendulum that measures the moments of our lives. It can be visible in our bodies, is sometimes even audible, and is a reminder of how consistently the body shows up for us and makes possible everything we love about these repeated trips around the sun we call life.

Without the breath I couldn't run after a kite with my son at the park. I couldn't sing or talk or hum, or whisper to someone special, "I love you." With no breath, not only is there no climbing, jumping, or dancing…but there's no life at all. Connecting to your breath is a great way to relate to the beautiful, mysterious, lifelong festival that is continuously going on inside your body: cells being born, flourishing, advancing, retreating, floating, dying, and recreating themselves again and again. Your body is a living being, and the breath feeds it something even more basic than food.

For a couple of years, I struggled with a type of asthma that sometimes left me coughing and gasping in the middle of a word. It also left me without the ability to breathe through my nose or smell even strong scents like onion or fish. Breathing through my mouth and worrying about when my next bout of coughing might strike, I was grateful for every single breath my body found. And when my sinuses began to clear and my nostrils opened for business again (my sense of smell returned from exile shortly thereafter), every day I thanked the breath, my nostrils, my sinuses, and my lungs, until eventually I forgot how desperately I had fought for my breath over those long months.

But we don't need to have a breathing crisis to be grateful for the breath. How are you breathing right now? Are your breaths long and deep, or short and shallow? Bring one hand to the center of your sternum and feel how the inhale lifts and fills your chest, and how the exhale releases your chest beneath your hand. If you have trouble feeling your breath at your chest, try putting your hand lightly over your mouth and feel the exhaling air leave your nostrils. Notice how effortless and steady your breath is. Your body is breathing for you all the time, taking care of you, filtering the air for you, feeding your brain and blood with oxygen, without you having to think about it or worry about where your next inhale is coming from.

Get curious about the breath. Notice how it feels when you bring your attention to the breath. What happens to your thoughts? Do your feelings change? Where does your attention go?

Place your hand on your heart and sense your breath. What do you feel? When you are aware of your breath, what happens in your mind? Notice too—what happens in your heart?

Give yourself the gift of listening to your breath throughout the day. Take a moment, bring your hand to your heart if that's helpful, and let your breath remind you of your aliveness. Let your awareness of the breath help you reunite with your body wherever you are.

10

Meet Your Inner Cheering Section

My son came home from school one afternoon and shared that in his PE class they were learning to run. As someone who would rather lie on a bed of nails than force my feet to circle a track, I tried to soften the wince that involuntarily squeezed my cheek as I turned toward him.

"We're gonna to be able to run a mile or more by the end of the year! Our coach says that if you get tired and you're not at the finish line, you can cheer yourself on."

Well. If you can cheer yourself on, that does change everything.

It's true—one of the hardest things for me about running is carrying the inner critic, who simultaneously drags her heels into the soft tar and yells in my ear, "Hurry, what's the holdup?" At other times in my life the inner critic felt like the crowd at the Roman arena, hordes of stinky thousands throwing insults and offal, all rooting for me to become the lion's appetizer at the feast. What if that crowd was cheering *for* me instead of against me? What if, when I'm lying with my face in the sand, the crowd knows just what to say to remind me that it's not over, that I am more powerful than I know, that the moment my legs stumble and shake is when I will find within me exactly what I need to leap up and keep going?

It's what I needed all along: a cheering section. Cheering myself on was exactly the opposite of what usually happened when life hurled moldy lemons at me. I had to transform the default mode of letting my inner critic rant about my flaws into drowning out my inner critic with a chorus of voices who want to see me smile.

My inner cheering section shouts things like, "Your body is worthy of love no matter what! You're doing a good job! This obstacle you just ran into headfirst is hard, but you can do it!" I know, they sound like the worst cheerleading chants ever. But they inspire me to dig deep when I've run out of shovels, and that's all that matters.

Close your eyes and imagine yourself in an arena where the crowd is cheering wildly for you. They want to see you succeed. They gasp when you fall, and encourage you to wipe the sweat off your brow and not give up. They believe in you, utterly. The crowd even knows that your worthiness doesn't depend on the outcome of any one battle—win or lose, you will be wiser for it. The crowd loves you no matter what; they don't care if you rip the seat of your pants or flub the most important speech of your life. You are their hero.

What words does your cheering section shout? What could they say to inspire you when taking the next step seems pointless? Give your cheering section exactly the words you most need to hear. Imagine your crowd, hear their voices, and let yourself take in their praises, their confidence in you. Let the crowd inspire you to remember who you really are.

11

A New Default

"Be kind to yourself. Be friendly toward yourself. Be loving with yourself." When I first heard these directives, they made me want to tear my hair out and go shrieking into the night. "Yeah, but HOW?! How do you be all nicey-nice to yourself?" I wanted to make a u-turn when my mind started to wander into the badlands of infinite suckiness, but I had no idea where to start.

One of my favorite authors, Anne Lamott, once said, "My mind remains a bad neighborhood that I try not to go into alone."[8] I needed a practice that could take me by the hand, lead me through the unfamiliar streets, and show me that the scary beings lurking in the shadows were unloved parts of myself that needed to be seen, forgiven, and even honored.

Loving-kindness practice, called *metta* or *maitri* in Buddhism, can become that guiding hand in the dark for you. Like all the practices in these pages, it takes time and consistency to make it a mode your brain defaults to in times of stress, instead of self-criticism. I find my mind switches on its loving-kindness practice when the freeway traffic leaves me running late, when my eyes have witnessed too many photoshopped pages of perfect bodies in a magazine, or when I wake up in the middle of the night to a seemingly endless review of where I've gone wrong in my life. As a self-soothing practice, loving-kindness rocks.

Buddhist teacher Pema Chödrön describes loving-kindness practice as cultivating an unconditional friendship with yourself.[9] You can also think of loving-kindness as a means of training the mind—inclining it in the friendlier direction you want it to go.

As a practice, it's very simple. You relax, invite a sense of warmth and love into your heart, and help it grow by inwardly repeating phrases toward yourself or others. Simple, and yet not.

Traditionally, loving-kindness is taught by offering phrases of well-wishing to yourself first. But for many of us, not loving ourselves enough is the whole point, so it can be great to start in a place where warmth and friendliness flow easily. I sometimes start by visualizing a little locket in my heart with a picture of my little-girl self in it. The photo I imagine was taken at two years old, on the first Easter I was old enough to look for eggs in our gravel backyard. In one hand I clasp an empty strawberry basket, and in the other I hold a colored egg up to my face, my wide brown eyes and the O of my mouth showing pure toddler awe. When I visualize this heart-shaped picture of myself, it's clear how deserving of love and kindness little Kimi is.

Another way to begin is to imagine someone who automatically makes you smile, someone whose well-being you wish for without reservation. Maybe it's your beloved grandmother (even if she's no longer alive), the pet who always seems to know when you need a cuddle, or the friend whose shoulder is always there for you to cry on. Find a place to start that's easy and natural.

The essence of the formal practice (which I'll take you through in more detail below) is that you offer silent blessings (you can call them aspirations, wishes, or phrases) in the direction of the person you're thinking of. The phrases can be very ordinary. One traditional grouping is: "May you be happy. May you be well. May you be safe. May you be full of peace." Or if it's to your child-self: "May I be happy. May I be well. May I be safe. May I be full of peace." Read through the steps and then try it yourself.

1. Sit or lie down in a very comfortable position. Use pillows or blankets to support you.

2. Breathe. Feel your breath and your body for several breaths. Place a hand over your heart if that's helpful.

3. Visualize someone whose well-being you long for: your child-self, your dear friend, or a loved one.

4. Let your warm feelings grow in your heart. See if you can generate a genuine warmth and friendliness toward this person.

5. Offer a blessing or aspiration phrase toward the other person or yourself with each breath.

6. When you feel your well-wishing strongly and fully, start to offer the blessings to yourself if you started with a beloved person, or to a friend if you started with yourself, and repeat steps 2–4.

7. (Optional:) If and when you feel ready, you can offer the blessing to friends, neutral people, difficult people, and all beings everywhere. Feel free to return to blessing yourself or your loved one at any time.

8. (Optional:) As you feel ready, offer the phrases toward your body: the parts of your body that are easy to like, the parts that are hard, and your body as a whole.

9. Slowly return your attention to the breath, and when you're ready, open your eyes.

Feel free to write your own phrases, to drop any lines that feel untrue, and to add the wording that resonates most in your heart. The point is to cultivate a sense of friendliness and love in your heart that you can direct toward yourself and others.

After practicing loving-kindness using the steps above, start reaching for the same phrases during your day when you step in dog poop, or open a nasty email, or get stuck in a sea of cars. Those moments when you can tell you're triggered, offer yourself (or your child-self) some loving-kindness as a balm to soothe your agitation and pacify your inner critic.[10]

12

Look for the Good

As human beings, we tend to go negative. Looking out into the world, we see the crumpled fast food bag in the street and the torn curtain in the window. Looking into the mirror, we see the pores, the pimples, the dark circles under our eyes. We see the freckles and miss the dimple, or we hate the dimple and miss the smile. Our eyes focus in on what's wrong. I've noticed it's hard to undo this tendency in myself, though sometimes if I'm open, the veil drops suddenly, and in a glance I can take in the beauty of the world around me.

Many years ago, my roommate and I made a three-day visit to the Polish city where we were to live for a year while we taught English to high schoolers. Arriving on the train, I was struck by the torn metal siding in the station and the crumbling rust of the ancient stair railings; once we were on the curb with our bags, my eyes took in the street signs, barely legible under dust and damage, and as we walked along the sidewalk the entire city seemed one blocky, stamped-out Soviet-era apartment building after the next. Neither of us spoke, but I felt sure my roommate's thoughts mirrored my own: This was where we were going to live? This worn foot sole of a town was going to be our home for a year?

At just the moment my mind headed in the direction of *I don't think I can live here*, a tiny bird flew down a foot or so in front of my shoes, hopping a few inches here and there to nibble the tops of a tuft of grass poking out of the broken concrete. I let my suitcase bump to a stop and watched. The bright saturated green of the grass, the pale orange stripe on the bird's beak, the angle of sunlight against the cracked sidewalk…it was beautiful. And at that moment, my heart gave a hopeful thump. There was beauty here, too. I only needed to look for it.

That scene proved to be a microcosm of how our year unfolded. Along gray and dingy streets, flowering jewel box parks spilled out onto the sidewalk. Amid the dusty carrots and beets at the street side vegetable stands, we found colorful miniature bouquets to take home to our fourth-floor flat. We found beauty wherever we were willing to see it.

As humans, we have a built-in bias to see what's not working, what needs fixing, what doesn't measure up. In general, it's not bad to see the negative—being on the lookout for potholes helps us avoid falling into pits. But seeing *only* the negative results in what I call "paper towel tube vision." When you look through the empty cardboard paper towel tube, you only see whatever shows through the little circle at the end of it, and nothing else. This is what we're seeing when we see only the flaws on our cheeks and only the crumpled coffee cups on the curbs of life. We see whatever shows in that little circle and lose all perspective. Seeing the good doesn't mean we don't see the bad. It means we throw away the paper towel tube, let our eyes take in what we don't like, *and* invite ourselves to see what's good there, too. We let ourselves see it all, the big panoramic view that acknowledges that we are more than any mistake or flaw or misdeed.

Imagine letting your mind unfold like a vast, exquisite map laid out on a table. Seeing the bigger picture can be an awesome way to see your body with more love. Can you see your body from the perspective of your whole life, of everything it has done for you and everything it will do for you, instead of just focusing on what isn't working at this moment? You are not just your face, not just your belly, not just some perceived blemish, some bulge or loose skin. You are not a list of things that "need" to be fixed by airbrushing, ab lifts, or regular avocado facials.

Make a habit of looking for the good. Catch yourself looking at the world—or at yourself—with a narrow, negative view. Then step back mentally and spread out your awareness. See with the eyes of your heart. Look for something that's working, something sweet, something lovely, something that opens you up. Look for the good in people, even people you wouldn't want to share a beer with. Look for the good in the mirror. Let looking for the good become a new default for you, and give yourself credit when you're able to hold whatever's happening with that big perspective and big heart.

13

Massage Yourself

I love massage. I've never been on a massage table and thought, *I hope this is over soon.* Instead my mind usually floats along in some variation of, *Wouldn't it be great if this lasted forever? Another few hours would be awesome....* If you've ever enjoyed a massage, you know about its many benefits, including relaxation, flexibility, and well-being. If you've never gotten one, what are you waiting for? Getting a massage from a skilled therapist can be an amazing way to show your body you care and feel more at ease in your own skin. Trading massages with a friend or partner can be healing as well. Let your muscles be touched and cherished. If you want to feel more comfort and connection with the skin you're living in, regular massage is one of the most effective ways to welcome yourself home in your body.

In between massages, as an everyday practice, you can give your body self-massage. Placing your hands on yourself with kindness tells your body it's okay, it's lovable, and it's good enough to be touched. Use warmed natural oils such as olive, raw sesame, coconut, or sweet almond oil—any edible oil your skin finds nourishing. Experiment with which oil works best for you. You can use the oil all over your body, before, during, or after your shower. Self-massage has been especially healing for me, allowing me to touch my whole body with love and compassion. My body finds it deeply reassuring on a cellular level, bypassing my old litany of judgments.

Self-massage sounds simple, but it's not necessarily easy. If you find the idea of massaging your own body challenging, I'm with you. For years there were certain parts of my body that felt like dead chicken skin when I touched them—my hands would freeze and then cringe away. It took many years of practice before I could touch every pore and crease with ease and reassure my body that every part of it was beautiful and worthy. So feel free to skip the parts of your body that are too hard to touch. It's better to massage what you can than skip the whole thing altogether. And be patient with yourself. As you begin, see if you can just say hello to the various parts of your body without judging them. Greet each elbow and knee and ankle in turn.

I do self-massage every day and have for years, and I can attest to the huge difference it's made in my tendency to blame my body for every little disappointment. Self-massage seems to get me and my body on the same team. When I go through periods when I'm traveling, especially camping, and I don't "do my oils," the old critical voices that point at my body and jeer start to creep in, whispering at first, then yelling full force. When I reunite with my daily oils again, the voices soon disappear into the ether.

It's wonderful to treat self-massage as a meditation practice, focusing on putting the oil on your body and staying with your breath, not believing any particular thought that happens by. You can also combine self-massage with loving-kindness practice, wishing yourself well as you massage the oil in all over. If you have a special mantra you find reassuring, one that reminds you of your true nature, repeat it to yourself as you massage. Use this one, if you'd like: "My body is worthy of love." Whisper it, shout it, cry it out.

Here is one way to practice self-massage:

1. In your bathroom, place a bottle of raw organic sesame oil in a bowl of very hot water.

2. Take your shower as usual.

3. As you get out of the shower, put a towel on the floor, and dry yourself lightly with another towel.

4. Pour some of the warmed oil into your hands and massage it into each part of your body, enjoying the breath and the feeling of warm oil on your skin.

5. You may want to sit for a while and let the oil soak in, or lightly dab your skin with the towel to remove extra oil, then get dressed as usual.

(Your towels may need to be washed in hot water to remove the oil residue.)

Try it for a week and see if it subtly changes how you relate to your body.

14

Couples Counseling for You and Your Body

What does marriage advice have to do with loving your body? Maybe you've heard of researcher John Gottman. He and his team do amazing work quantifying what makes relationships last. By watching just a few minutes of an argument, they can tell more than 90 percent of the time whether a couple will stay together.[11] According to Gottman, in order to feel like our relationship is a happy one, we need to have at least five positive interactions for every one negative interaction. (An interaction can be just a word or a touch or even a glance, and can be positive, negative, or neutral depending on whether it's received generously, met with hostility, or ignored.) If the ratio changes to four positive interactions for every two negative interactions or worse, we unconsciously start to look for the big exit sign over the door.[12] Our human brains need a lot more positive interactions than negative ones: we're sensitive to negativity, which makes us irritable in a relationship and can give rise to a cascade of dissatisfaction that leads to divorce.

We're also resilient to negativity—just five positive interactions and we start feeling more optimistic about our partner. Much to my relief (and I'm sure yours), this means we don't have to be perfect. We can say the crabby word, get frustrated and mad, and heal later on with small acts of kindness that bring us back into balance. Can you see where I'm going with this?

When I first read about this concept, a lightbulb switched on in my head. If I'm in a "relationship" with my body, how many positive interactions do we have for every negative interaction? If I start the day yelling at my thighs for how my jeans look, then deprive my stomach of anything but celery sticks, then punish my legs with a painful workout, and later binge on potato chips after eating almost nothing all day…hmm. Did I have ANY positive interactions with my body? No wonder I spent so much of my life wishing I could break up with my body. And my poor body must have dreamed every night of a sweeter, less fault-finding partner than me.

What about you? How many times a day do you appreciate your body rather than criticize it? Do you have at least five positive interactions for every one negative interaction? For most of us, the answer is clear…we have a huge deficit of positive interactions with our bodies, and an overabundance of negative ones.

But the good news is we can turn it around. Notice how often you criticize your body and what words you use. You can lower the number of negative interactions by decreasing their frequency, interrupting them, and replacing them with positive interactions.

When I find myself (even after years of learning to love my body) having an "I hate my body" moment in the mirror, I start with an apology: "Oh body, I'm sorry. I shouldn't have said that. It was mean. I take it back. Let me make it up to you." And then I remind myself of the many things I like (and even love) about my body: *My hands have long fingers that remind me of my mother and grandmother. My smile is welcoming and covers my whole face. I like how big and wide-spaced my eyes are. I like my feet; they're steady and strong, and they take me amazing places. And my elbows have never caused me a bit of trouble, ever.* By the time I've gotten through all of that, I've moved past whatever bad feelings I had toward my body. We're back on the same team.

To create more positive interactions with your body, answer the following questions:

1. What part of your body causes you the least pain and difficulty?

2. What part of your body has given you the most enjoyment in your life?

3. What part of your body reminds you of someone you love or respect?

4. What part of your body helps you engage in your passion or take care of those you love?

5. What part of your body do the people who love you say they find beautiful, comforting, or appealing?

(If you don't like a question or have trouble answering it, make up one of your own until you have a list of at least five things you like about your body.)

Now, when you catch yourself in a negative interaction with your body, counteract it by repeating to yourself the five things you like about your body. Memorize this list and use it to become a better friend to your body, one you want to share your life's adventures with, whether climbing into a tree house, building a tree house, or painting the tree house of your dreams.

15

Affirm and Aspire

Do you remember that Stuart Smalley sketch on *Saturday Night Live* from the last century? He looks into the mirror and says, "I'm good enough, I'm smart enough, and doggonit, people like me!" Personally, I find it hard to use affirmations without thinking of this send-up of "positive thinking." If affirmations work for you, that's wonderful, and I have some suggestions about how to work with them effectively. If affirmations slide off you like an egg on Teflon, don't worry: there are these other things called aspirations which can sneak in beyond where affirmations fear to tread. Instead of saying, "I love this beautiful body," you can say, "I hope someday I can love this body and think of it as beautiful."

Affirmations can be hard for me. They often feel inauthentic, like trying to convince myself I can fly when it's perfectly clear I left my imaginary wings at the cleaners. An aspiration is softer, reflects a genuine desire, and is a great place to start out when we know where we want to go but aren't sure how to get there. What do you want for your body? How do you *want* to feel about your body? Aspirations give a voice to these inner longings.

Below are some ideas to figure out whether affirmations or aspirations might work best for you.

A. Affirmations: Can you look into the mirror and say, "Hey, beautiful!"? If so, you'll probably find it helpful to work with affirmations. Great! Read on. (If you find saying "I'm beautiful" kind of hokey or false, skip to B.)

   Choose or invent an affirmation that strikes a chord for you and embodies the love you want to have for yourself and your body. For example, "My body is a beautiful temple I am blessed to live in." Write down your affirmation and repeat it to yourself. If you find this phrasing of affirmations to be too strong, go to B. If you find it too weak, go to C. If it's just right, go to D.

B. Aspirations: If affirmations seem forced to you, try the aspiration practice instead. Pick an affirmation you wish worked for you, then write the words "May I come to believe" or "May I come to see" in front of it. As in, "May I come to believe my body is a beautiful temple," or "May I come to see myself as worthy of love no matter what." You can take any affirmation and change it to be more aspirational and less forced. I personally find that my mind rejects affirmations the way vinegar rejects oil, but if the same wording follows the phrase "May I…," my mind doesn't raise so many objections. If you want to step into a wild variation on affirmations, read C. Otherwise, go to D.

C. If you tried A but want something stronger, try these "level 3" affirmations, which are more radical and outrageous. Phrase your affirmation in a big, wild, all-encompassing way: "My extraordinary body is the life force energy of the universe's power embodied as me. In its tremendous freedom, it chooses to manifest as anything, and it chose me!" Or, "I am made of pure light. I embody the universe's creative force of life, which flows through me and all beings. The atoms and energy that make up this amazing body have always been part of the universe and always will be." Let your level 3 affirmation capture your imagination and fill your heart. Exclamation points are a plus! Read some Walt Whitman or Maya Angelou or Rumi for inspiration. Proceed to D.

D. Post your affirmation or aspiration in different places in your home, car, or office. Write it in your calendar. Make it your screen saver. Turn it into a piece of artwork. Schedule and send yourself emails reminding yourself of it. Draw it on your vision board. Repeat it to yourself as you hold each bead on a prayer bead *mala*. Recite it during your meditation practice. Write it on your yoga mat. Find other creative ways to integrate it into your life. Change, refresh, or rephrase your affirmation or aspiration as needed.

Feel free to visit my website at http://www.kimberyoga .com/52-ways-to-love-your-body/aspiration-affirmation-phrases/ and print out the aspirations there or use or adapt the following phrases:

All bodies are lovable. My body is lovable.

Today, may I be a good friend to my body.

May I see beauty in myself as I am.

My body is my best friend.

My body is perfect in its imperfection.

May I learn to love my body just as it is.

My growing love for my body supports me and the liberation of all beings everywhere.

16

Inner Critic Game Plan

I've often wondered what potent combination of childhood characters my inner critic represents. She's the voice of the playground bully, the sadistic coach, and the back-stabbing popular girl, all rolled up into one shrill package. From puberty until long after I'd left the schoolroom behind, she stalked me from the grocery aisles, to the line at the post office, and all the way into the toilet stall, looking for any little excuse to persecute me. Ordinary activities like walking past my own reflection and sitting down to eat provoked her into a body-shaming frenzy.

As I grew older, I started to get curious about my inner critic, learn to identify her, and notice what triggered her worst behavior. It's helpful to think of her as a voice distinct from my own—to recognize her voice not as my own, but as the voice of opinions about appearance that I had swallowed and digested. She was society's voice, internalized so that I could inflict any potential judgment on myself before even stepping off the front porch and into the world's slings and arrows.

Before recognizing her, I hardly even heard the criticism as a distinct voice: I experienced it as "the voice in my head," the one I identified with completely. What she thought, I thought. What the voice believed, I believed. Every horrible thing she said about me must be true. It was the only voice I knew, or at least the only one I paid any attention to.

By noticing my negative thoughts about my body and identifying them as "my inner critic," I could start to listen to another voice in my mind, a quieter one that was consistently reassuring and comforting rather than reactive and full of complaints. I learned how to not take my critical voice as the word of God, and instead take the wise counsel of the voice that reminded me of my best self, even when I was lying flat on my face. It turned out to be a big improvement over kicking myself when I was down.

Notice your own negativity around your body. A study by *Glamour* magazine showed that 97 percent of women have at least one "I hate my body" moment every day.[13] The average number of these negative thoughts per day is thirteen, but some women report hundreds. At my worst, I could have competed for the Guinness World Record for "Most Negative Thoughts Thunk."

First, notice for yourself if you have "I hate my body" and/or inner critic thoughts, and how often. Do you find these thoughts helpful? Do they make life easier and more enjoyable? For most of us, it's the opposite. Personally, I find it exhausting to try to control my inner critic when she goes into full fire-hose mode. If you're having trouble recognizing your inner negative voices, simply recall the last time you stood in front of a dressing room mirror trying on clothes at the store. That chorus chiding you about what doesn't fit and why, and how you look standing in your underwear between changes: those are the voices I'm talking about. Wouldn't it be amazing if you left them on the other side of the door while you tried on that new sweater?

Here's another question that's hard to contemplate but well worth asking: What could you accomplish in your life if you didn't have to wrestle with your inner critic? What would you do with all that extra energy and time?

Below is a practice (inspired by Pema Chödrön's "four Rs"[14]) for noticing and letting go of your "bully" voice around your body. You can do it anytime and anyplace.

1. Recognize: Notice the negative voice and what it says to you in all of its creative ways of expressing what's wrong with you. When it comes up, notice whether you're tired, or sad, or stressed. Notice what actions it tells you to take (go on a diet, exercise more, and so on).

2. Refrain from acting or planning to act on this voice's advice.

3. Relax: Breathe into it and observe it; invite some space around it.

4. Remind yourself that you don't want to believe this voice any longer.

5. Repeat a phrase that you find comforting, one your kind inner voice uses.

6. Resolve to do this again and again, whenever the negative voice comes up.

17

Get Mad, Set Boundaries

Y ou know what makes me mad? Hearing about little kids
in elementary school feeling pressure to diet even before
they can spell the words "insane" and "idiotic." You know what
else I can't stand? Those freaky pop-up ads on the internet for
"One Secret to Lose Belly Fat Fast." Really? Fuck you very
much, body-hating scammers. And the thing I hate most of all?
The giant liposuction billboards you sometimes see when
driving down the highway, that I swear must be designed to
make even the thinnest woman wonder if she should shatter an
entire herd of piggy banks to get her thighs vacuumed off.

Does my anger make you uncomfortable? For a lot of us,
especially women, because we weren't allowed to express anger
in our families of origin, much of our anger gets channeled into
sadness instead. As a little girl, crying because I wasn't allowed
to go to the same party/overnight/troop meeting as my sister
meant I would be comforted and reassured, or at least treated
like I was a normal kid who was feeling down and needed time
to commune with her support group of stuffed animals. Anger
at the same disappointment meant I would be treated as if I

were an irrational and somewhat dangerous lunatic who might start throwing knives at the wall at any moment. It was not normal, and I was not okay.

We can end up believing that rage is unspeakable and cringe-worthy, something we turn away from in others and try to repress in ourselves. As a result, we unconsciously spend a lot of time polishing a veneer of understanding and niceness on top of the tightly closed chest of our anger. Notice if this is your tendency. If body-negative messages make you feel sad instead of mad, know that it's fine for sadness to be your default response instead of anger. At the same time, try to recognize, explore, and embrace your anger, which otherwise can build up in the body and heart. In her book, *Healing Rage*, rage expert Ruth King encourages us to listen to our "rage child" who needs to be heard, loved, and held.[15] My friend Kathleen shared with me that as a child she once heard her scientist father explaining the biological reasons why women were physically inferior to men. She channeled the fire of her anger into a deep appreciation of what her body was capable of and all the ways it performed better than the male bodies around her. Can you channel your anger in a positive direction of change in your life? Let your anger guide you to a kinder relationship with yourself, even with the most difficult parts.

What gets your blood roiling about body image in our culture? Tapping into anger can help us to firmly say no to those forces that would have us stay stuck in body negativity and yes to those that inspire us to love ourselves fully. Consider the following:

1. How do you feel about the fact that a narrow definition of beauty, which less than 5 percent of women naturally fall into, is imposed on 100 percent of American women?[16] (A similarly narrow definition of male beauty is becoming more prevalent every year.)

2. *Our culture brainwashes young women and girls into thinking that their natural bodies are not acceptable and that they must control their bodies and discipline themselves to live up to a nearly impossible standard of beauty, all while being told their attractiveness is the most important thing about them.*

    Is this statement true or false? If true, what are some of the consequences of this message in society? And how does this statement make you feel on a scale of "It doesn't bother me" to "It's outrageous and wrong"?

3. Have you thought much about the message we receive in our culture that some bodies are more lovable than others? Why do so many of us believe that message? Who has the right to tell you how you are allowed to feel about your body?

4. How often during the day are you exposed to media and societal messages that you aren't good enough the way you are? How does this affect your energy level and how you feel about yourself?

5. Who profits from us hating ourselves?

If after answering these questions you're feeling kind of mad about how our culture manipulates us around body image, contemplate the following:

1. How can you channel this anger to protect yourself from these messages? What are three things you can do to resist and reject body negativity in your life?

2. These messages are hostile to your mental, physical, and emotional well-being. How is protecting yourself from them a form of self-compassion? How is resisting these messages an act of kindness toward yourself and others?

Let yourself be angry about how bodies are treated in our society. Then set in motion the change you want to see by starting with how you treat your own body. Designate your body as a hate-free zone, and do all you can to make the world a safer place for all bodies, no matter what they look like.

18

Accept What's Hard

When I was a kid I was always confused by the expression, "Life is not a bowl full of cherries." Duh, of course it's not a bowl of cherries: it's not necessarily easy, enjoyable, or sweet. Sometimes we go through long periods where nothing resembling "cherry-ness" can be found. Even a bowl of cherries isn't a bowl full of cherries.

When you stop at a roadside stand during the short and precious week of cherry season and buy a bag of dark red beauties, get them home, and roll them into a bowl where they are ready to eat one at a time—even then, some of the cherries are perfect, tangy, and sweet, while others are sour, mushy, or squished from traveling under their companions during their trip from the orchard to your kitchen. You have to look at every single one and decide whether to eat it or not. And even after you've carefully inspected the particular cherry you're about to bite into, it has—like every last one of them—a pit you could break a tooth on.

Loving your body is not a bowl of cherries. Loving your body doesn't mean you will never have another "I hate my body" moment or that somehow you will magically love all the parts of yourself you once despised. There will be days we see nothing but pits and rejects. I still have days when I wake up and wonder if my thighs could use a little tough love and whether I should give up eating anything that tastes good. I expect to have days like this until my days run out. What's changed is that every day used to be mostly pits. Now the bad days are the exception rather than the rule.

When I first started learning to love my body, I shifted away from wanting to have the perfect body to unconsciously wanting to have the perfect relationship with my body. In this fantasy, my body and I make friendship bracelets and flower chains and hold hands as we skip off into the sunset, and everyone looks at us and sighs, "If only I could have a relationship with my body as awesome as that." Yeah. Never gonna happen.

What I learned is that a relationship with my body is a real relationship, one where I get irritable and say mean things sometimes, one where my body and I have screw ups and miscommunications, one where at times I want to throw my hands up in the air and call it quits. Bad body moments happen, and they probably always will. It's a real relationship that I work on all the time, but it's never going to be perfectly smooth. The upshot is: if it feels hard to love your body, that doesn't mean you're doing it wrong. It's gonna be hard sometimes.

What is hard for you to accept about your body? What do you wish was different? Acknowledge what you don't like. Be real about it. How you feel about this part of your body may never change. And it doesn't have to. We have places where we feel stuck, but that doesn't mean anything about who we are. It doesn't make us wrong or bad.

Accept your difficult places. They're yours, so own them.

Then ask yourself the question, how do I want to treat myself? More kindness, less meanness? More enjoyment, less criticism? Make lists of what you want more of and what you want less of.

Keep nudging yourself in the direction you want and away from the direction you don't want. Treat yourself how you want to be treated, *even though you have places where you're stuck.* Even though you have places on your body you're certain you'll never think about with affection, keep going anyway. As you strengthen your ability to treat yourself with friendliness when it's easy, sometimes that strength will spill over into the places where it's hard. Sometimes it won't. Sometimes you'll get so into the habit of turning down the negative voices that you'll automatically override them when they pop up, even around the places that are toughest for you. Expect ups and downs, twists and plateaus, even times when you fall flat on your face. Expect bruises and scrapes, and have some Band-Aids and ointments ready. Expect the pits and you'll enjoy the sweet-juicy-tangy goodness even more.

19

Get Real

In *The Velveteen Rabbit*, the Skin Horse explains what it means to be real: "'It doesn't happen all at once,' said the Skin Horse. 'You become. It takes a long time... Generally, by the time you are Real, most of your hair has been loved off, and your eyes drop out and you get loose in the joints and very shabby. But these things don't matter at all, because once you are Real you can't be ugly, except to people who don't understand.'"[17]

So which do you want? Do you want to be perfect, or do you want to be real?

There are two basic definitions of perfect, one imaginary and one based on real life. Imaginary, ideal perfection is mathematic perfection—the infinitely long, perfectly straight lines that exist only on paper and in our heads. Ideal perfect inflicted on the human body becomes those images we have plastered to the insides of our heads (thanks, media!), images that have been photoshopped into a perfectly symmetrical, flawless, and unattainable standard of beauty. Ideal perfection leads us on an exhausting chase where we pull products off shelves and follow the next aging expert's directions in our attempts to suspend the inevitability of time just a few inches away from the surface of our skin.

Real perfect is different. Real perfect means "good enough," as in when I ask you, "Can I set the groceries here?" and you say, "Perfect." Real perfect can also mean that something is fully, wholly, completely itself. You are perfect because you are already fully yourself—and you always have been.

Ideal, mathematical perfection doesn't exist in nature and isn't compatible with life. A perfectly round sphere exists only in one place…your imagination. How great would it feel to let go of this unreasonable standard of perfection that is impossible to meet or maintain?

American writer Nathaniel Hawthorne told a story about a scientist and his beautiful wife, whose only flaw was a birthmark on her face. The scientist wants her to be perfect, so he sets himself up with his beakers and flasks to find a solution to remove the blemish forever. And in the end he finds just the thing, a medicine that removes the birthmark, but kills her in the process. She dies, but hey, she's perfect![18] When we throw ourselves into the pursuit of physical perfection, we forget that removing the flaws from something sucks the life out of it.

Ideal Perfect: An infinitely long, perfectly straight line

A perfectly round sphere

A mathematical proof

A photoshopped image that eliminates all scars, pores, and stretch marks

Real Perfect: The asymmetry of a tree

A beloved, tattered stuffed animal

The ocean and its mix of calm and wildness

The moon with its craters and bumps

A child's toothy smile

When we look at a tree, we can see both its imperfections and its beauty. Maybe it has too many branches on one side, or is bare and straggly in places, but it's perfectly itself. We can see what's beautiful in its imperfections. You're like that: perfectly imperfect. We're not meant to achieve imaginary levels of perfection. We are meant to be fully ourselves.

In Sanskrit, the word for perfect, full, or whole is *purna*. Purna doesn't mean idealized perfection, but perfection that comes because something is fully itself. You are wholly yourself, and you always have been, with all your strengths and weaknesses, talents and flaws, successes and failures. By this radical redefinition of perfection, you are perfect now and always have been.

Why not redefine perfection for yourself, and give perfect a definition that includes you as you are?

Look at the categories on the previous page: ideal perfect and real perfect. Which category does your body fit into? Can you define perfection in a way that includes yourself, that makes space for a real, beautifully flawed human life? What resistance do you have to thinking about yourself as perfect already?

Don't worry; seeing yourself as perfect doesn't mean complacency. We can be perfect and still change and grow and learn. Instead of trying to fix our brokenness or imperfection, we come from the place of knowing that we are good enough already. Get real—dump the idealized version of perfection and give yourself permission to be flawed, wonderful, messy, and very human. Perfect.

To write your new definition of perfect onto your bones, post this aspiration someplace and repeat it as a mantra: "May I see myself as perfect, with all my flaws and beauty, just the way I am."

20

Turn Off the Comparomatic

Does your mind default to its "comparomatic" setting— where it sits around and compares your body to the people around you? Maybe it starts enumerating the superior qualities of your coworkers, your friends, your neighbors, the guy sitting in the coffee shop, the woman on the magazine cover. And then, when our minds don't have anything to compare ourselves to, we compare ourselves to...ourselves: *I used to be able to run five miles, what's wrong with me today? Why am I stiffer than yesterday? I never used to forget my friends' birthdays, but now I can barely remember my own.*

It's easy to get squashed in the gears of the comparomatic. It starts the moment we walk out the door into the world, switching on without us even noticing. We look at someone and unconsciously note: Is this person fatter than me? Thinner than me? Richer than me? Smarter than me?

Everything is fuel for the comparomatic. We compare ourselves physically, emotionally, energetically. We compare our cars, our hair, our homes, our jobs, our partners, our families, our education, our clothes; even on our yoga mats we compare how close our heels come to the floor in Downward Dog. Just the other day I caught myself looking at a photo online and noticing the gorgeous living room in the background. *My house isn't that nice. Why don't I live in a house like that?* The internet can be a giant trigger for "comparing mind," switching it on remotely, right in the comfort of our own homes.

Your mission is to turn off the comparomatic…no more comparing your body and your life to others'. Comparing ourselves to others sets the ball rolling on a Rube Goldberg machine that traps us in a small, unkind view of ourselves and the world.

What does comparison energy feel like? When you are caught up in comparing yourself to others, does it help you feel happy, satisfied, like you're enjoying life? When I get caught up in comparing mind, I find my life always falls short. I see people doing things I wish I were doing, having more fun, getting more recognition. What does this evoke? Envy, sadness, upset, irritation. Comparing mind adds a low level of constant stress and dissatisfaction to our lives.

But there's no point in giving ourselves a hard time about it. We're hardwired to compare, and our culture encourages it as well. We make decisions about how we should behave based on what we see others doing. It's part of our socialization and our ability to conform to a civilized society. It's not altogether bad—if we see people treating each other respectfully, we compare and adjust our behavior, and are more likely to treat others kindly, too.

The problem is that we spend most of our time comparing our interior life to others' exterior lives. My interior life is messy and strewn with seemingly insurmountable obstacles. By comparison, other people look like they really have their shit together. To paraphrase Steven Furtick, it's always a mistake to compare someone else's highlight reel to your behind-the-scenes bloopers.[19]

Notice your casual judgments of yourself and others. Notice what situations rev up the old comparomatic and how your mood shifts when it starts up. Notice what's there, and let yourself feel the stress that arises when your comparisons and judgments are going strong. Noticing the tendency to compare is our main tool for shutting the comparomatic down.

Try looking at your life without comparing—just being yourself and letting others be who they are, without judgment, without ranking yourself above or below them. Imagine how your life would be if you did this. How would it feel? Would you be able to relax into and enjoy your life and your relationships more? Would it free up some emotional space and allow you to let go of those stories that prevent you from stepping into your life fully?

Try this exercise:

Get comfortable and close your eyes. How good would it feel to let go of some of the things you compare yourself to? Think of something in your life that you compare yourself negatively to. For just this moment, let go of that comparison. Label it untrue and unfair and beside the point. How would it feel to let go of just that one comparison? Let it go now. Why not? Let it go and see how it feels in your heart. Let go of it whenever you feel it coming up. Let go of it over and over on each breath. Let it dissolve back to wherever it came from.

21

From Self-Discipline
to Self-Devotion

Which would you prefer to have residing in your body: a ferocious jungle cat, or a loving friend? It turns out, if you want to tame the jungle cat, it helps to throw away the whip, the chair, and the chains first. Research shows that people who practice self-compassion, an inner sense of understanding and kindness toward themselves, report less depression and anxiety and are *less likely to overeat*.[20] Surprise! It turns out loving-kindness practice really works. Being friendly instead of critical toward yourself helps you develop more resilience, balance, and optimism.

Years ago I ate lunch once a week at my favorite Indian buffet. The serving table would be piled high with fragrant curries, spicy *daal*, and fried vegetable fritters. I felt like a hungry tiger at feeding time; my rule was that I could only go through the buffet one time and have a little of everything. Otherwise I would just keep filling my plate and eat until my stomach hurt; then I'd feel miserable and mad at myself for the rest of the day.

My appetite was a dangerous tiger at the end of a heavy chain that only firm self-discipline could control. When I told my yoga philosophy teacher, Carlos Pomeda, about my buffet dilemma, he showed me how to rethink my tiger's appetite. Carlos said, "Isn't it wonderful that you can go to a restaurant you love, get all the things you like, enjoy your meal, and take good care of yourself by eating just enough so your body feels good for the rest of the day?"

I was stunned. His words turned my world upside down. Instead of a starving tiger, I was just me, being kind to myself, noticing what my body needed, and providing for those needs in a way that acknowledged my well-being. My restraint could demonstrate a sense of love toward myself, not the need to control myself with an iron will. Since then, instead of self-discipline, I aim for *self-devotion*.

Whatever rest, food, and exercise you offer your body, do it out of love. Connect to why it's important to take care of yourself: *I'm eating well because I want to show my body I care. I do exercise my body finds fun because I want to enjoy my body. I rest when my body needs to rest because I trust my body's signals.*

Self-discipline is harsh, sharp-edged, and unconcerned about your overall well-being. Self-discipline ignores everything but the bottom line.

Self-devotion is juicy and enjoyable. Self-devotion encourages you to listen and pay attention to your body. When you approach yourself with a friendly, forgiving attitude, your "failures" are no longer demonstrations of your inadequacy, but just part of being human. You can stay open to yourself and return to the desire to love and take care of yourself no matter how far you might have gone astray. Be that good friend to yourself, and you'll achieve a sense of inner support and affection you never imagined possible. You'll always feel at home.

Where in your life do you feel like you have to use a lot of self-control, or be hard on yourself just to maintain a baseline of okayness? What's the story that you tell about yourself: "I have a weakness for… I have trouble saying no to… I'm out of control when it comes to…"? Reframe the story in terms of self-devotion instead of self-discipline: "I let myself fully enjoy a piece of cake because it's delicious and I know that the more I enjoy it, the less deprived I'll feel." Or, "I eat what my body's craving and push away the plate when I'm full because my body doesn't want to overeat." Or, "Eating when I'm hungry and stopping when I'm satisfied isn't about willpower. It's about loving myself so much that I can't imagine doing it any differently."

Write your self-discipline story, then rewrite it as a story about acting out of self-love. Remind yourself of this new way of looking at yourself whenever that situation arises. You can turn your tiger into a cuddly house cat by treating it with love.

22

A Good-Bye Party

Sometimes the myths and stories we tell ourselves about our bodies cling to us for dear life. They pop up again even after we've tried to let them go, like a bad prom dress we keep finding at the bottom of the closet. Didn't I get rid of that years ago?

There are three steps to deal with this: Look, Learn, and Let Go. Look means shining the light on our internalized stories. Make a list of all the myths you hold about your body… bellies aren't sexy, fat women aren't lovable, if I eat bad food then I'm a bad person, I can't be beautiful unless I fit into a certain size jeans, blah, blah, blah. When you think of another one, add it to the list, and keep adding, even the absurd ones. Yup, take every ugly stereotype, every hurtful insult, every unsaid thought about your body, other people's bodies, all bodies; bring them up from the dredges of your mind and put them down on paper. This process can be painful, but think of it as an exorcism. The unknown, the unconscious, is often more powerful in our lives than the conscious. By bringing our unconscious assumptions to the surface, we make them less scary, more known, more familiar. They start to lose their power over us.

Then Learn: disprove each one of them, through your own experience and education. One of my myths was that big butts weren't sexy. An experience that helped me disprove that myth happened at the drugstore. While buying dental floss, I saw behind the cash register a display of "Booty Pops": pads you put inside your jeans to make your butt look bigger. My mind floundered for a moment. People buy things to make their butts look bigger? Yes. Because they think it's sexy!

Some myths are more challenging to disprove. How about the myth that fat is unhealthy? We often hold on to this one even though we know (or are) fat people who exercise and eat well. Nutrition researcher Linda Bacon's book, *Health at Every Size: The Surprising Truth About Your Weight*, helped disabuse me of my belief that being fat and having fat is a terrible thing. I'll let her speak for herself:

> That "obesity kills" has been the backbone of the federal public health campaign. Yet that is not supported by evidence examined by federal employees. Their research found that "even severe obesity failed to show up as a statistically significant mortality risk" and suggested that overweight may actually be protective.[21]

The point of the Learn step is to look at our own beliefs and be willing to challenge them, to read things that upset the ideas we cling to, and to look at our bodies anew. Disprove each one of your myths to your own satisfaction. Some may take longer than others. Be patient.

Now we can get ready for step three: Let Go. Take a good look at your list, however long it is. Take a moment to feel compassion for your body. It's not just carrying baggage, it's carrying truckloads of judgments and criticism. No wonder it gets so tired out.

Create a ritual in which you symbolically throw these beliefs away:

1. Find a rock along the beach, and write on it some of the myths. Throw it as far into the water as you can. When these beliefs pop up again, remind yourself that you've already thrown them away.

2. Create a bonfire (or even light a candle in the middle of a roasting pan), write the myths on a piece of paper, and burn them. Watch the smoke curl up toward the sky, and when you catch yourself believing one of your old myths, remind yourself that they are every bit as insubstantial as the smoke and ash they turned into.

3. Compost your list of myths, tear it up, mix it with chicken manure, feed it to your plants. Chop it and

mix it up with water in the blender, and pour it down the drain. Use it as bedding for your rabbit or bird.

4. Write out your myths on colorful pieces of paper, tear them up into little bits, and throw a good-bye party for them! Notice how beautiful they look all torn up and mixed around, transformed from something harmful and unseen into a beautiful, mixed-up celebration of letting go.

Be creative. The more meaningful you make the discarding of your myths, the more you'll feel that you've let go of them for good.

23

Make Your Own Rules

Bodies carry our clothes, our bags, and sometimes heavy boxes or children on our hips. Our bodies also carry our enjoyment, our worries, our injuries, and our rules about who we are and what our bodies mean in the world.

I used to live by the unspoken rule that my body was unlovable and would never be good enough. That rule was like an old tattered shirt I wore and never took off, not even to sleep or shower. No matter how beautiful I might have looked to anyone else, no matter how happy I appeared for the moment, that rule lay underneath it all, closer to my heart than even my skin.

Who made that rule? And who made the rule that I have to believe it and let it decide whether I'm allowed to appear in a swimsuit at the beach? What kind of jerk would make a stupid rule like that anyway—someone who thinks I should only ever make love in the dark so my sweetie won't see my stretch marks?

The person who would make a rule like that is someone I would walk in the opposite direction from at a cocktail party. If I wouldn't rely on this person's advice for whether or not the guacamole is worth eating, why would I believe him about something as important as how I feel about my own body? No one has the right to tell me my body isn't worth loving. Not the media, not Hollywood, not the rude guy at the gym, and certainly not the weight loss surgery billboard on the freeway. Not even the voice in my head that whispers, *You'll never measure up. There's something wrong with you.* It doesn't get to make the rules either.

We don't need anyone to tell us how to feel about our bodies. There's no International Body Image Police out there, telling you that you have to hate where your thighs touch, or loathe the scar on your cheek, or despise the fact that one breast is larger than the other. We internalize the rules and then force ourselves to live by them, often without ever looking at why we agreed to live by those rules to begin with. And it doesn't even matter why. What matters is deciding that from here on out, you make the rules. You're the one who gets to decide what the rules are. Proposed first rule: My body is worth loving just the way it is.

Make new rules. We gave up the old rules in the last chapter. Now ask yourself, what rules about bodies do you want to live by? What rules about bodies would make the world a better, safer, more loving place for all bodies? Take a sheet of paper and some colored markers, and make a list of the new rules you want to believe about bodies. Find rules that resonate with you—that you feel excited about embracing. Here are some to consider:

Love a new body every day. Celebrate all bodies.

Touch and be touched.

All bodies are worthy.

Beauty comes in all sizes.

Eat lunch. Don't skip lunch. Bodies need lunch.

Love your body no matter what. Loving your body doesn't have to have anything to do with how it looks.

Make your own list. Put it in your wallet or hang it up on your mirror, and when you find yourself reciting one of those old shriveled rules, pull your new rules out and remind yourself that you and your body don't live by anyone else's rules anymore. You make the rules now.

24

Inner Demons? Invite Them to Tea

There's a story about how Buddha spent several days, weeks perhaps, in a cave meditating, while the demon Mara and all his nightmare minions harassed Buddha from outside the cave's entrance. "You're nothing but a lump of camel poop," they shouted at him (I'm totally quoting). "What makes you think you'll ever become enlightened? You're a worthless good-for-nothing, more ear wax than brains, wasting your life away for naught. A pathetic failure as a prince AND a monk. If only your father could see you now." Their eerie laughter twined around Buddha's limbs and set doubt working in his heart. The unseen faces unnerved him, and he felt conflicted: should he leave the cave and venture into the darkness? If he gave up his efforts, he would be rewarding the demons for theirs. He sat in the dim light of the fire and watched as the smoke curled up in tendrils, drifting out of the cave opening. Stirring the coals with a stick, he saw steam rising from his teapot and was struck by a sudden inspiration.

"What ignorance makes you think you will succeed where all others have failed?" Mara's haunting voice echoed across the cave walls.

Buddha took a deep breath. "Mara, is that you?" He waited a moment, hearing only silence. "Mara, the tea is ready. Won't you come in and warm yourself by the fire? Come have a cup of tea."

Now the versions of the story diverge. In one variation, Mara, shocked by Buddha's friendliness and lack of fear, flees, minions in his wake, his power to terrify gone. In another version, Mara comes in, sits next to Buddha by the fire, and they converse. Buddha, seeing Mara in the flesh, realizes that to Mara, taunting Buddha is just a job, nothing personal. And Mara by the fire holding a cup of tea isn't so scary after all.

Invite your demon in for tea. Seriously. How often have we cowered in fear from the judgments of the inner critic? You're feeling just fine, about to stop in at your favorite café for a coffee, and you look down at the way your jeans bunch up on your legs and find yourself adjusting the waistband a little lower or higher, to no avail. Your jeans don't look right, and whose fault is it? Before you know it, your inner critic goes into over-drive, demanding drastic diets and self-flagellating exercise, and you find yourself sitting at a table in front of an artificially sweetened black coffee instead of the caramel milkshake you'd been dreaming of all day. Why does the inner critic have such power over you? Why does she have a hotline to your unworthiness?

Get to know her. What does she look like? Whose voice does she speak with? And why is she so freaking pushy?! No, actually don't ask that...yet. But set up an imaginary meeting with her, ask her some neutral questions, be a little friendly. Stay curious, even if she doesn't know how to be anything but mean at first. You might be surprised by what she looks like when she comes out of the dark. Find out her *name*.

Your first meeting with your inner critic:

1. Find a comfortable and private place to sit with your journal. If you like, have a cup of tea and a snack nearby. You can make a cup of tea for your inner critic as a peace offering.

2. Sit quietly with your eyes closed, and invite your inner critic to tea. Ask her to come sit; ask whether she'd like milk and sugar in her tea.

3. Imagine her sitting across from you, or simply write in your journal something about what she looks like. You might notice some interesting or surprising things about her appearance. Ask her name, and how she's doing. Ask her about her job. Tell her you've noticed

she's really good at her job. See if you can see her as just a person (or part of yourself) with a job to do.

4. Open your eyes and write down any insights this exercise brought you in terms of how you see your inner critic, or how you can relate to her. We'll get to know her better in the next chapter.

25

Inner Demons Love Cookies

W hen I first started doing lots of yoga, I pushed myself hard. I shamelessly (but subtly) competed with whoever was on the mat next to me, pulling myself harder into each forward bend as if the enlightenment trophy was going to be awarded to the most hardworking yogi at the end of class. If that didn't take me past my edge, I competed with myself, all to the inner chorus of *Come on, Kimber, don't be such a wuss. Change hurts! Suck it up.* You can imagine the inevitable results. I injured myself. Not once, not twice, but over and over. *That teacher was bad*, I thought. *I'm never going back to that class again.* Eventually I ran out of teachers to blame, and I stumbled into a late-arriving epiphany—I was hurting myself.

Hearing the story of Buddha and Mara (see previous chapter), I started to get curious about my inner pushy voice. Whose voice was it? Where did it come from? Immediately I suspected my stern Marine colonel grandfather whose approval I never earned. Or my middle school softball coach who pretended he was a Marine colonel. Or, even more likely, my inner anorexic, in her full glory, skinny as a rail, anxious with hunger, tanned to rawhide perfection, cheeks gaunt, lipstick perfect, glaring at me in utter distaste down her too-narrow nose.

Rolling out my yoga mat, I lay down, closed my eyes, and contemplated. For the first time ever, I called to my inner demon, "Come out, come out, wherever you are...." Never before had I asked the voice to come to me: it had always arrived unbidden, unwelcomed, right at the moment I needed to ease up, telling me to push harder. I imagined myself at the table of a cozy little cottage, a tea setting with thick mugs and cookies in the center. The faint sound of footsteps crunched on the pathway outside, and I nervously rose to answer the door. I took ahold of the knob and pulled the door open. For a moment, I thought I'd made a mistake. This was not my inner anorexic, or my grandfather, or any character from my past. This woman was tall, huge, dressed in a tight seventies-style blue sweat suit. Her hair was pulled back severely from her face into a tight blonde-gray ponytail, her cheeks reddened from the cold. She barely glanced at me as she strode through the door, intent on warming herself around the cup of tea and sampling the cookies.

I sat down and watched her in amazement as she settled into her snack. Her name, it turns out, was Svetlana, and she was a Russian gymnastics coach. I hadn't done much gymnastics as a kid, but as a Russian history major in college, I had a deep love for all things Russian. She had somehow emerged fully formed from my unconscious. Slowly, understanding dawned on me. She wasn't trying to make me look like her, or be her. Pushing me hard was her job, that was all. She'd much rather be here enjoying cookies and tea by the fire than standing in a drafty gymnasium yelling at me and furtively taking swigs of vodka from her flask. She had her own weaknesses, failings, and resentments, having nothing to do with me. For all these years I'd taken her voice as *the* voice of authority in my life, and in my yoga practice, and why?

"Svetlana, thanks for coming to tea," I said. "Can you please use a quieter tone of voice from now on? And by the way, I'm not going to listen to you as much anymore." Raising a pale eyebrow, she shrugged her shoulders and nodded her thanks, grabbing one more cookie on her way out the door.

The next time I found myself in yoga class, I felt the familiar urge to pull myself into a deep forward bend using excessive force and insufficient respect for my back. Briefly, the interior of the cottage flickered in my mind, and I heard Svetlana's sneakers crunching up the path. Her hand rattled the doorknob for a moment. Taking a deep breath, I waved the image away. Letting go of the pose briefly, I settled into an easeful version of the forward fold with relief. I could practice alone on my mat. Svetlana could have the night off.

Try getting to know your demons. See if you can understand more about what motivates them and what their own dreams are. See if this exercise can help you see them with more distance, perspective, and empathy.

26

Give Your Inner Demon a Vacation

How do your inner demons like their tea? What's their favorite: muffins, scones, or doughnuts? Svetlana, my inner demon/gymnastics coach, loves a strong Russian tea and has a particular weakness for those little packaged madeleines you can buy at the counter at the local coffee shop. Give her a package of those, and she's perfectly happy to settle in and chat for a while. Observe your inner demons. What do they look like? What motivates them? What is stuck up their butts?

Set the stage. Where are you meeting? At a sunny park, at a bustling café, or in a peaceful living room? You're welcome to use my cozy little cottage from the previous chapter. Let your imagination go, and be surprised at what you find. Once you and your inner demon(s) have taken a comfortable seat, just listen to her/him/them for a while. Ask her probing questions, like you're interviewing her for the *Rolling Stone* magazine cover article of the year. Be objective and interested. This is your unconscious you're talking to; you can mine some really juicy stuff!

Then it's your turn. Take a deep breath and tell your inner demon what you need from her. "I need you to chill out. I need you to be nicer to me. I need you to turn down the volume, and the drama." Tell her why. Even enlist her help. "I need your help in treating my body with more respect. I want to be better friends with my body, and I need your support." Address any concerns she might have. Reassure her that you're not ditching her, you just need her to tone it down.

Suggest a getaway in an exotic locale…where do demons like to go on vacation? Depending on how long you've struggled with your inner demon, she probably hasn't had a vacation in years, possibly decades. She has *a lot* of vacation days saved up. And no, you won't change the locks while she's gone, but she'll have to live by a few ground rules when she gets back. No more put downs, no more undermining, no more punching bag. Set firm boundaries. Explain to her that she is entitled to her opinion about things, but that you won't be taking her advice as much. If she looks at you skeptically, assure her that while it might take some time for you to tune her out, you're set on your path of transformation.

Call a truce. No more war on the body, no more war on your self-esteem, no more war on your well-being. By the time you've listened carefully to your inner demon, she feels acknowledged and validated; you might be amazed at how reasonable she can be. Tell her you're glad to have met her, wish her a good trip, ask her to send you a postcard, and show her graciously to the door.

Congratulations—you've met your inner demon face to face and lived to tell the tale. But this is just the beginning. Perhaps after this initial meeting you'll find your internal radio picks up the inner critic station less and less, as if you're driving out of range of the transmission tower. Some days the station might come in loud and clear, and some days it might be full of static. Be patient. Our old habits of self-criticism don't dissolve easily. Let them dissolve one drop at a time.

27

Your Sassy Inner Best Friend

To successfully deal with your inner demon in the long run, you're gonna need more than tea parties. Demons don't play fair. You need someone who's got your back. This is a job for your inner best friend.

My inner best friend is a diva. Glamorous, ageless, voluptuous, jaded but kind. Compassionate *and* hilarious. She thinks I'm gorgeous, and knows exactly when to whisper that reminder in my ear. She thinks anyone who disagrees with her on this point is an idiot and will proudly tell them where their head is stuck. She's an endless source of ricocheting zingers (never directed against me, always designed to amuse or wake me up) and prefers to be referred to as The All-Encompassing Goddess. She loves cupcakes with pink frosting and iridescent sprinkles. She is shameless and will get me choking with laughter in no time flat.

Close your eyes and imagine your inner best friend. What does she (or he!) look like? Where are you seeing her, in your mind's eye? How does she greet you? With a hug, a kiss on the cheek, a squeal and a spin? This best friend already knows your secrets, wouldn't dream of betraying you, and listens to you, nodding and comforting, for hours. She sees your beauty and strength, and is ready to remind you of your best self whenever you forget. She remembers your secret triumphs and your deepest wounds, and is ready to cheer or console as the mood requires. She tells you your detractors are long-tongued, babbling gossips (mine is fond of quoting Shakespeare) and assures you there's no reason you should take it personally.

Your inner best friend doesn't put up with self-pity for long. She's compassionate, but won't let you wallow in negativity. She can be piercingly honest, clearing away the bullshit and letting you know she loves you the whole time. Trust her to know your heart. Trust her to defend you against inner and outer insults and injuries. She knows the pen is mightier than the sword and that to laugh and walk away is sometimes the most powerful stance of all.

Imagine all of your most idealized best friend qualities, embodied in one being who lives in your own head. She's with you all the time, everywhere; you only have to remember her to invoke her comforting presence. When your inner demon acts up, breaks the rules, or smashes the china, introduce your best friend, and let her set the boundaries and wave her magic wand. You might be surprised: she may have tricks for dealing with your inner demon you never dreamed of. Get to know her, and vow to be pinky-swear-hope-to-die-BFF-blood-sisters. Make up a secret handshake. Then, when your inner demon isn't satisfied to wait outside the door, ask, what would my inner best friend do? And proceed knowing she's got your back.

28

Forgive Your Body

Our bodies sometimes throw us for a loop. We get injured, we get old, we get pain in weird places. We become ill or disabled, or we just…change. Everything was going along fine and then, out of blue air, the body betrays us.

Puberty can be a real game changer. *Here I am, enjoying my body, having fun being a kid, just starting to understand a few things about life, and boom! Breasts! And what?! Hair in my underarms? And hips?! What are they for, other than attracting obnoxious attention? And don't even get me started on the whole bleeding thing—I didn't sign up for this!*

Many other events and conditions alienate us from our bodies—a cancer diagnosis, infertility, addiction, molestation and abuse, weight gain and loss, menopause, trauma from oppression—the list goes on.

In almost every film, there's a moment of dramatic tension when something difficult or terrible happens—a misunderstanding, an accident, a loss—and the rest of the action is spent exploring the effects of that rupture. What was that moment for your body? The moment when your mind and your body declared war, or simply diverged silently and sullenly along different paths? It's good to pinpoint the pivotal event(s), even if we have removed ourselves so far from our body's story that we've forgotten why we feel alienated.

If your body were your best friend, how would you handle this betrayal or disappointment? Hopefully, you'd sit down with your friend and talk it out. It would go something like this: You take a seat, cup of tea in hand, tissue box nearby, and finally tell your friend why you're so pissed at her. She listens for a while, maybe she defends herself, maybe you argue some, maybe even harsh words are exchanged. You listen to her side of the story, and then you both cry, both apologize, both pledge to not let misunderstandings muck up your relationship any longer. Your relationship, you both discover, becomes stronger as a result.

What is the difficult conversation you've been avoiding with your body? When I journaled a dialogue with my body around puberty, this was the result:

Me: I was happy just being a kid, eating whatever I wanted, not thinking about what I looked like, and you started to change me into a woman, without asking me anything about it! I was so mad at you. I didn't want breasts, I wasn't ready to bleed, or think about sex, or worry about whether my stomach poked out too much. But you didn't care, you just went on like what I wanted didn't matter! You're so selfish…I hated you!

Body: I hear you that you didn't want to change. But I couldn't help it…it just happened. It was kind of exciting and kind of scary. I needed you to help me through it, to be excited and scared with me, to help me figure it all out, but you were just mad all the time. I was so hurt and lonely. Right at the time I needed you most, you totally ditched me, and were suddenly mean to me, hurting me all the time because of something I had no control over! You abandoned me.

Me: Oh my god, I had no idea. I completely forgot about how you might feel. I'm so sorry I wasn't there for you when you needed me. I really missed all our good times together. I know it wasn't really your fault. I'm sorry I was so mad at you. Can we start over?

Body: I'm sorry that it seemed like I didn't care about you. I do care about you—I always have and always will. I missed our fun together, too! I'd love to start over with you.

[Me and Body cry a little bit, and hug, and decide to do something fun together.]

If you have a painful relationship with your body, you can start to heal it by airing your grievances, sharing your hurts, and then listening to your body's point of view. Use your imagination to come to a place of understanding and forgiveness between your body, mind, and heart.

29

The Second Arrow

W hat do you see when you look in the mirror? What story do you tell yourself about your body? Many of us, when we see our reflection in the mirror, think, *Ugh. When will I get rid of these* [insert most hated body parts here]*?!* Then we silently (or not so silently) vow that tomorrow we are starting a new diet/new exercise program/new strategy for excising those parts of our body forever. Later, when we're driving, or washing the dishes, or talking to a friend on the phone, we're still giving ourselves a hard time about it—sometimes for hours or weeks.

"There are two arrows," Buddha told those gathered around him in the forest grove. "The first arrow is pain, injury, loss. You can't avoid it. What you can avoid is the second arrow; the one you shoot at yourself. The second arrow is the story you tell yourself about why you got shot by the first arrow to begin with."[22]

When you hear about the second arrow for the first time, you might be as surprised as I was: "I don't have to shoot the second arrow? I don't have to tell and retell the story about how there is something wrong with me? Or with the person who hurt me? Or with the world?" Nope. That's the suffering we create for ourselves. You don't have to tell the story that makes you or the world bad.

Here's an example: my partner comes home late from work. I'm mad, because I had dinner ready forty-five minutes ago, and she didn't even call to tell me she was running late. Her being late is the first arrow. The second arrow is the story I tell myself: *What a complete, inconsiderate, self-centered jerk! I can't believe I married her. What's wrong with me that I always end up with people who treat me like a doormat?*

Then I shoot a few kerosene-soaked second arrows at her, too. Add a little PMS to this flammable mix of arrows, and we can end up in an epic, hours-long fight involving slamming doors, threats of divorce, and multiple emptied tissue boxes.

But what if I didn't shoot the second arrow? What if my story went like this instead?

People are late sometimes and forget to call, despite their best efforts. I'm bummed she got home late. Maybe she's bummed, too. I know she loves me and would never do this on purpose.

First arrow but no second arrow. Pain but no suffering. Disappointment but no argument.

When you look into the mirror, what's the first arrow? Your body. Your aging, changing, un-airbrushed body. Your body *is what it is*. It's not bad, and it's not necessarily even painful. It's just a body.

But looking in the mirror, I might compare my thighs to some youthful model's that I saw on a radio station billboard. Squinting at my reflection, I remind myself that my lips are nothing like Angelina's and that even as a teenager, my body did not look like an airbrushed model's. The longer I look, the crappier I feel. Comparing myself negatively to someone else is a second arrow by itself. Then I get out the big artillery: the story I tell myself about why I don't look "better." It starts with, *What's wrong with me that I don't look younger/thinner/more gorgeous?* and moves to, *I need to work out more and do a master cleanse—that will get me started.* Soon my inner anorexic feels her powers return and she helpfully suggests, *Stop eating.* Uh-oh.

To stop shooting the second arrow, notice when you start comparing. Your body stands alone. Your body is good and worthy. Heck, it's carried you around your whole life, and for its thanks you compare it to Hollywood actresses, or your friend, or yourself ten years ago? Get real and give it a break. Notice when an encounter with the mirror (or the scale—a different sort of mirror) sets your inner critic on a raucous binge of self-hatred and diet fantasies.

Get to know your second arrows. When one of them pops up on your bow, ready to sail into your heart, gently remind yourself to put down the bow. Or if the arrow is already headed your way, duck. And if it's already hit you, place a hand over your heart and offer yourself some compassion. *Ouch, that hurts. I'm so sorry.*

And when you find yourself shooting the same second arrow over and over again, observe how it feels in your body and in your heart. Offer it your breath, and a sense of spaciousness and tenderness. These stories can be powerful and persistent. Notice it, hold yourself with kindness, and remind yourself: they're just stories. Put down the second arrow. The first arrow is hard enough.

30

Tell Your Body's Story

I f your body could write its own autobiography, what would be the stirring climax? The moment of white-knuckled terror? The heart-warming conclusion? If your body's story was made into a movie, would it be an action-adventure film? A romantic comedy? A disjointed black and white experimental film that only an art student could love?

Let's start with the good stuff. You and your body have been on some amazing adventures together. What are your best memories in your body, your most enjoyable experiences of being embodied?

Three moments stick out for me, among many: (1) the feeling of aliveness surging through my entire body the first time I successfully hula hooped with two hoops in my backyard garden; (2) playing with yoga poses on a wet beach during a spectacular sunset, when my mind stopped thinking and my whole being just savored the delightful experience of embodiment; and (3) my first orgasm, with a lover in college, the feeling of "Wow, Body! What was that?" and the delicious answer, "THIS is what the fuss is all about!"

Contemplate your most enjoyable experiences with your body, with play or athletics, when feeling warm rain on your face, swimming in the surf, getting a mind-blowing massage, eating a sun-warmed strawberry straight from the field, enjoying a sense of well-being and ease on vacation or with a loved one: any time you've deeply appreciated pleasure, agility, freedom, or fun in your body. The act of childbirth inspires many women to feel empowered and even humbled by their body's capacity for transformation. Having sex and feeling sexy can evoke an overwhelming sense of gratitude toward our bodies and a deep appreciation of our own aliveness. When have you felt most at home in your body?

Hold each experience in your mind and heart. Remember what it felt like to be in that moment. Invoke the feeling in your body...your body remembers. Offer your body a sense of gratitude for that experience, no matter how long ago or how fleeting the moment was. "Thank you, Body, for making that moment possible. Thank you for being on this journey with me. Thanks, Body. You rock." Repeat to yourself whatever words of gratitude feel most resonant.

Reminiscing about the good times and thanking your body for making the wonderful moments in your life possible helps you realize that you already have the foundation for a good relationship with your body. Instead of believing the occasional thought that the body is a rusty ball and chain that hobbles you, you remember that your body has already proved itself to be a loyal and steadfast friend who has crossed every chasm with you and explored every joy.

Holding your body with gratitude for all you've been through prepares you to listen to your body's story of your future together: how to be happy and healthy. Your body probably has a lot of great ideas—are you ready to hear them? Listen to your body like a trusted friend. Listen by getting quiet, asking questions, and tuning in. We often already know what our body wants from us, but we don't always pay attention and respond the way our body needs us to. Read through the steps and the questions for the contemplation below and then begin the exercise as you feel ready.

1. Quiet your mind by listening to the breath.

2. Hold one of the questions you want to ask your body in your mind and ask it.

3. Listen quietly and wait for an answer. Sometimes it's helpful to write the answer down before asking the next one.

Hi Body, how are you? (Start out easy…)

What do you need from me?

How can I be kinder to you?

How can I be more loving?

What do you want me to know about you?

I want to work with you. (What does your body say in response?)

Notice if it's easy or hard for you to hear the voice of your body. Listen and keep trying.

31

Feed Yourself with Love

What does your body love to eat? Have you ever *asked* your body what it likes to eat? When I ask my body, images of fresh veggies float through my imagination: warm curries, sautéed greens, asparagus roasted in olive oil, diced avocados. Then big mangoes wander by, followed by juicy peaches, tangy raspberries, and sweet blood oranges. And apple pie. And croissants. And all kinds of yummy things.

Sometimes it's hard to hear what your body wants because your mind gets into Cookie Monster mode: *I want chocolate now. Donuts now. Chocolate donuts. Now.*

Then the mind spends a lot of time strategizing about how to get its emotional fix, the oh-so-brief stress relief that a heavy dose of sugar and fat provides to the brain. But when I ask my body—my best friend—what it wants, it almost never says chocolate donuts.

In fact, it took me years to realize that my body dislikes donuts and has trouble with concentrated sugar in almost all its forms.

Every time I ate sugar, I turned irritable and crabby. For years I thought I hated birthday parties—halfway through the party I thought, *Party games are stupid. Birthdays are stupid. Look at all these wasteful decorations, and don't even get me started about the paper plates. Don't my friends have anything better to do than pollute the earth with more trash?* I turned into a raving party-pooper bitch. Finally I realized if I skipped the cake or ate just a bite, I liked birthdays just fine: I could blow my party horn and enjoy stumbling through the three-legged race along with everyone else.

Your body may not react to sugar the way mine does; I hope not. But how *does* your body respond to different foods? Do you pay attention to its reactions? What foods help your body feel full and sated? What foods make it irritated and upset?

Check in with your body and ask it how it likes different foods. How does a vanilla milkshake feel? How does a colorful salad feel? How does a beautifully presented, lovingly prepared meal feel? How does it feel to eat fast food behind the wheel of your car?

A great exercise is to go to the local farmers market, close your eyes, and ask your body what it needs, what it wants, what it craves. Go around to the different stands, take in the sights and smells of fresh vegetables and fruits, and invite your body to respond with a "No, thanks," a "Yes, please," and the occasional, "Oh yeah, baby, I need some of that!" You're not shopping for what you think you *should* eat, but learning to listen to your body's voice. Slowly you'll develop an ear for your body's own preferences and wisdom.

Different foods have different effects on your body. Notice whether foods make you feel satisfied or depleted, energized or fatigued. Note whether a certain food makes you feel clear-headed or fuzzy, happy or irritable, easeful and content or bloated and uncomfortable.

Keeping an eating journal where you write briefly about how you feel before and after meals can help you tune in carefully to what your body loves and what it complains about. Remember, you're not keeping track of calories, just noting how you feel before and after eating.

Even knowing what our body enjoys most, we sometimes eat things that disagree with it. When I do this, the tendency is to give myself a hard time...*I knew better, what was I thinking? Now I've ruined my day with this stomachache.* Giving myself a hard time is as helpful as banging my head against a concrete piling. Instead of knocking myself around, I've learned to apologize to my body: "Oh, poor body. I'm so sorry for ignoring what you needed. I'll remember for next time that you really hate it when I don't stop eating when I'm full. My bad. I'll listen more carefully from now on. We're in this together."

Would you purposefully give your best friend a stomach-ache? Never. Give your best-friend body what nourishes it, feeds it, and honors it. Learn to listen to your body's intuition and enjoyment, and you'll find that your body returns love to you like jackpot coins from a slot machine.

32

Listen to Your Body's Cravings

H ave you ever thought to yourself...?

If I listen to my body, it will tell me to lie prone on the couch and eat chocolate-covered potato chips until I can't move.

If I trust my body, I'll never make myself go to the gym again and I'll devour pints of Ben and Jerry's like they're peanuts.

If I pay attention to my body's needs, I'll become a boneless sloth with nothing to live for.

If I love my body, the skies will rain blood, birds will explode for no reason, and the world will get sucked into a cosmic death spiral to the tune of Queen's "Bohemian Rhapsody."

Is it true that your body has the personality of a lazy, ravenous, good-for-nothing wastrel who only cares about watching Wile E. Coyote finally catch the Road Runner? I used to think so. I was pretty sure that if I listened to my body I would succumb to a mint-chocolate-cookie-ice-cream-induced coma for the rest of my days.

The first time you listen to your body feels like standing at the top of a ridge and trusting the air to catch you and cradle you safely to the earth below.

It's a scary and exhilarating leap of faith in yourself: that your body's wisdom exists and you can trust it wholly. Every fear shapes itself into a looming doubt to keep you from jumping and knowing the truth about yourself.

Here's the truth:

1. Your body is an animal.

2. Your body knows what makes it feel good.

3. Your body loves to move and eat and rest.

4. Your body doesn't want to overeat or undereat.

5. Your body doesn't want to be injured by too much movement or too little movement.

Your body wants to feel good. Let it show you what it needs. Let your body catch you.

I used to think that I was the kind of person who couldn't control herself around food. If I started eating a candy bar, I finished the whole thing. I figured that listening to my body meant I wouldn't stop with just one candy bar; you'd find me in a heap of chocolate-smeared wrappers at the bottom of the box.

Imagine my surprise when, after listening to my body for a while, I learned that it doesn't like candy bars. My body feels irritable and tired when I eat a whole nougat- and caramel-filled vending machine snack. Nowadays my body says, "One cookie would be perfect. One piece of that chocolate bar would be delicious. Half a truffle is just right."

For years I rolled my eyes at people who said crap like that. Really? You can stop at half a truffle? Bullshit. Not me.

Yeah, me.

You, too.

Here's a good place to start. Below is Linda Bacon's "Live Well Pledge," a list of aspirations that invite you to listen to and trust your body:

Today, I will try to feed myself when I am hungry.

Today, I will try to be attentive to how foods taste and make me feel.

Today, I will try to choose foods that I like and that make me feel good.

Today, I will try to honor my body's signals of fullness.

Today, I will try to find an enjoyable way to move my body.

Today, I will try to look kindly at my body and to treat it with love and respect.*

Seriously, does this look like a recipe for bedsores? No way. This is the recipe for being able to eat what you want, when you want, as much as you want, and no more than you want; for moving your body in ways that it loves; and for treating yourself like a goddess—not like a caged tiger.

For me, loving my body is the recipe for feeling the best I've ever felt in my life, for enjoying food more, for being in better shape than I've ever been…and not by forcing myself to do things I hate, but by letting my body do what it loves.

Your body is the fount of tremendous wisdom. Are you ready to listen?

* Excerpt from *Health at Every Size: The Surprising Truth About Your Weight* © 2010 by Linda Bacon.

33

Relish Your Pleasure

A friend of mine named Dr. Bliss studies people who enjoy eating food more than other people do. What does that mean? Imagine joining a pleasure guru at a multicourse meal, someone who oohs and aahs over the colors and textures, the careful preparation, and the riot of flavors, and through witnessing this person's unbridled enjoyment, your enjoyment and the enjoyment of everyone at the table increases immeasurably. Most of us would love to eat with a person like this, just because it would make for a fun and memorable evening we would talk about at cocktail parties for the rest of our lives. "Our mission," Dr. Bliss says, "is to recognize that when we enjoy our food we not only absorb more nutrients and feel more satiated, but we inspire those around us to do the same. It makes the meal more satisfying on every level."[23]

That's right: when we enjoy our food more, we get more physical and emotional benefits from our meal and perhaps eat less than people who don't enjoy their food as much. I know—this goes against almost everything we're taught about food.

We're supposed to eat broccoli without butter, salads with low-fat dressing, and watch out for sugar! But eating a fat-free, sugar-free, flavor-free diet is a recipe not only for no longer enjoying food, but also for feeling continuously hungry and getting caught up in a pattern of cycling between eating no cupcakes (ouch) and ALL the cupcakes (double ouch).

Instead, what if we relished, savored, and enjoyed the hell out of our food? If we're going to eat it anyway, why not get the maximum dose of pleasure from it? Eat beautiful food, taste and smell every last bite of it, moan with delight, and see how your body feels. Say no to food that isn't pleasurable. See how it feels to trust in your body's pleasure, to know that it will deposit you happily on the doorstep of satisfaction. Here's an exercise to grow your skills as a brand-new pleasure guru:

1. Buy a bar of your favorite chocolate.

2. Find a relaxing and enjoyable place to sit, maybe outside in the sun or on a favorite chair in your home. Privacy is good.

3. Open up your chocolate bar and break off a piece.

4. Pause and breathe. Look at it. Notice its texture and color. Notice if your mouth starts to salivate in anticipation.

5. Bring it close to your nose and sniff it. Savor and enjoy the smell. Notice if your mouth and body seem eager and excited or disappointed or something in between.

6. Gently bite off a piece with your teeth. Let it rest on your tongue and melt a bit, then start to chew it. Let yourself make audible sounds of enjoyment if you are enjoying it. Moan. Close your eyes and let all the different flavors and sensations roll through you.

7. Swallow, pause with your eyes closed, and feel the remainder of taste and smell sensations that are still present, but fading, in your mouth. Notice if you feel the urge to eat the rest of the piece. If you want the rest, follow the same process. If not, save the rest to eat later.

How was it to eat the chocolate so slowly and deliberately? Notice if you feel satisfied. Notice if you want more. How might your habits around eating change if you intentionally enjoyed all your food this way?

34

Not All Hunger Is for Food

What are you truly hungry for? What does your body crave that isn't food? What nourishes your heart?

You know that moment when you get to the top of the big rock you were climbing and you look out over the vista, and your soul says, "Ahhhhh." Your body and your heart and even your mind chime in, "Ahhhhh." Every part of you hums with amazement, as if every cell is appreciating through its own particular sense the wondrous view. Some of us have this experience in a museum, perhaps left in tears on a bench surrounded by a series of Georgia O'Keeffe's flowers and sinuous landscapes—it happened to me. Some of us feel full-body ease and pleasure listening to—or making—music. When have you had moments like this? Can you make time in your life to feed your soul this way?

I used to be hungry all the time. I was hungry before meals, after meals, during meals, and between meals. The only time I wasn't thinking about food was when my mouth was full.

Curling into bed at night, I fell asleep thinking about breakfast cereal and yogurt. Hunger dominated my life. And for years I thought hunger was all about food. But really, that growly, empty sound in my belly was the only signal from my body that I listened to. Just like how we learn to respond to a friend who answers emails but not phone calls or texts (guilty!), my body learned there was only one blip that showed up on my radar: hunger. But the truth was that it didn't want just food. It wanted play, and affection, and time to get lost in the forest. It wanted to dance and belly-laugh and feel that creeping sense of awe that sneaks up on us when we see the sun rise out of the fog, and to be overwhelmed by the gorgeousness that sometimes pops out from around a corner. My body wanted to feel everything—and be seen as beautiful as it was.

But I wasn't listening. All I heard was: HUNGRY. And I answered: FOOD. It took years of pausing and tuning in and paying attention to hunger and all its subtle variations to slowly learn that my hunger wasn't all about food.

Your body, heart, and soul need more than food to thrive. Ask them right now what they are hungry for. See if any of these ways to feed your soul appeal to you:

1. Connect to the earth: get your hands into some garden dirt, walk through mud puddles in your bare feet, or spend time breathing in the air of the forest.

2. Draw on yourself: offer the words your body most wants to hear, especially reminders to see your own beauty.

3. Make a love your body altar: put items on a shelf or mantle in your house that remind you of how you want to relate to yourself and feed yourself with more love.

4. Make love your body art: get butcher paper and have a friend trace your body and color it in with designs and words that inspire you. Another idea: get out the finger paints and let your hands and toes have some messy fun.

5. Follow your dream: write, dance, learn to skydive, connect with friends, camp in the desert. Live your way into your heart's desire, and your body will be grateful, too. There is nothing your body wants more than your happiness.

35

Invite In Good Experiences

The world is full of potentially triggering experiences and altogether too many people with ready put-downs about our bodies that say more about them than they do about us. For me, idly picking up a fashion magazine at a nail salon can induce an all-day headache and diet-filled reveries. I call it Post-Airbrush Syndrome: when looking at too many perfectly photo-shopped bodies causes your brain to melt. Negative body moments can happen anywhere, anytime...when someone comments on what we're eating (No, this isn't lowfat yogurt, why do you care?), when someone asks if we've lost weight (What, you thought I could lose a few pounds?), or when none of our clothes seem to fit right (Did I leave everything on high heat in the dryer again?!). Bad body moments sneak up on us and, if we're not careful, can fill our days and our lives. The inner critic likes to stockpile these moments and use them as ammunition to convince us that we don't have the right to feel good in our bodies.

We can disarm our inner critic by seeking out good body experiences. Spend time with people who love you and your body, who readily welcome your body into their space and admire your glow. Do things you love that make you feel fantastically alive. Invite experiences that make your heart tremble with joy and longing.

Once, on my first visit to a Japanese-style public bath, I saw a group of three older women sitting on low benches in front of bowls of water they were pouring on each other. I watched them lean over one another, whispering into each other's ears and affectionately scrubbing each other's backs. Their beautiful bodies were full of wrinkled skin and rolls of fat, and my eyes did their best to linger on (without staring at) the lovely scene they made. Their easy friendship and the warmth they showed each other filled my body with a longing to be touched and cherished. The picture in my head of the three of them—bodies sprawled, their unself-conscious pleasure in each other's presence—is indelibly marked on my mind, sending my body and heart the clear, unimpeded message that my body (and yours) is worthy of connection, love, and belonging, no matter how much my butt pooches over the edges of the wooden stool, no matter how many wrinkles join my cellulite and stretch marks. This is the vision I conjure up to answer my inner critic's demands for antiwrinkle facial care products and fad diets.

You can't always predict what the ingredients are for a good body experience, and sometimes things go awry, but you can place yourself in the way of one by intentionally seeking it out. Here are some ideas to inspire you:

1. Look into the mirror with love: toss your hair, look over your shoulder, blow a kiss, shake your head, and say, "You look gorgeous, darling. We're going to have a great day together."

2. Visit a hot tub with friends with the intention to love your bodies as they are. Take turns scrubbing each other's backs or massaging each other's feet.

3. Get a massage and enjoy every minute of affirming touch.

4. Schedule an appointment with a professional photographer (or a friend with a camera), get dressed up in your favorite clothes (or undressed), find a fabulous location, and pose away! Take the best shots, get them framed, and hang them where you can enjoy them.

5. Reserve a day for body love. Ask your body what it wants to do and plan the whole day around what it loves most: maybe breakfast at a café, a yoga class, a trip to the beach, time with friends, a homemade meal from the farmers market, and dancing—or an early bedtime. It's a twelve-hour date with your body.

36

Love Your Body Yoga

My body and I became best friends on my yoga mat. It helps that my body loves yoga. In fact, if I don't show up on my mat during the day, it gets crabby and irritable. But when I find my way into my first Downward Dog and let the muscles in my arms and legs stretch and extend, my body whispers, "Thank you." Sometimes it replies in all caps and with lots of extra punctuation: "THANKS, KIMBER!!!"

Here are a few simple poses that can feel wonderful for your body and don't require a mat or lots of time. Try them and see how your body likes them.

1. Cat/Cow Pose

    a. Come to your hands and knees on the floor. Feel free to place a folded blanket under your knees for cushioning.

    b. Take a big inhale and lift your head up high so that your neck is outstretched and your head is facing forward. At the same time, let your belly release toward the floor.

c. Now, as you exhale slowly, lower your head between your arms and arch your back up toward the ceiling. Continue inhaling and exhaling, moving smoothly with your breath, five to ten times. Notice how it feels in your spine and your chest.

2. Hip Turns

a. With your hands and knees on the floor, now begin to move your hips in a small circle. It may feel like more of a side-to-side motion at first. You can let the circles get larger, but try to keep your arms straight. Then slow, stop, and switch to circle your hips in the opposite direction.

b. If you want to try a fun variation, see if you can move your hips in a figure eight, and then switch to the opposite direction.

3. Child's Pose

a. With your hands and knees on the floor, draw your two big toes together so they are touching and spread your knees farther apart. Sit back toward your heels and let your forehead rest on the floor if possible.

b. Let your arms rest on the floor alongside your ears, or let them rest back alongside your body if that's more comfortable.

c. Take several long breaths here, and see if you can allow the breath to fill and expand your rounded back.

d. This pose can be very restful and enjoyable; it's also a great place to check in with your body and ask it how it's doing and what it needs from you.

37

Go Natural

W hen was the last time you felt grass tickling the spaces between your toes? When did you last swim in a natural pond, or skip rocks across a lake, or feel sand pulling under your feet as the waves poured over them? Sit among the roots of a tree, lean your body against its trunk, and feel the breath entering your lungs expand your back against its bark. Notice how your body feels sharing air with the branches and leaves. Remember that your body belongs to the earth every bit as much as the roots beneath you do.

Our bodies are nature, every bit as extraordinary as the most soulful range of mountains or the wildest waterfall. We forget that our bodies are as natural as rain when we spend more time with our devices than we do with tomatoes and moss and birds. Look at "the narrowest hinge" on your hand, that smallest knuckle on your pinky. Recall Walt Whitman's words: that knuckle "puts to scorn all machinery."[24] Hold out your pinky and watch as you curl it open and closed. The Good Gray Poet had it right…that top knuckle of your little finger is a miracle of evolutionary engineering that we still only dream of inventing technology to imitate.

Your fingers unfurl just like the frond of a fern, like the curl of a wave on the ocean, like the cone of a shell formed grain by grain under the surf. Sitting in nature, my body remembers that it is at home, that it belongs here, that it is an inseparable part of this messy, lively world.

Here are some ways to remember your true nature and enjoy your body in the outdoors:

1. At the beach: Use your feet to make messages in the wet sand. Bury your legs in the warm, dry sand. Play tag with the waves. Take a nap in the sun. Build a castle at the edge of the water and invite a friend to smush it with you when you're done.

2. At the park or meadow: Take off your shoes and let your feet explore the different textures of earth and green. Roll down a grassy hill. Do a cartwheel. Skip. Lie on your belly and watch the ants weave back and forth. Climb a tree. Make a chain of flowers and wear it.

3. In the snow: Have a snowball fight. Build a fort. Lie down and make a snow angel. When your toes and fingers get cold, run inside and drink something hot to warm yourself up from the inside out.

4. In the garden: Taste different herbs and flowers. Mix some of them together and see how they change each other's scent. Dip your nose into flowers and sniff

deeply. Water the plants with a can instead of a hose and feel the weight of the water as it pours into the earth. Dig your fingers deep into the soil and feel all the temperatures and textures. Cup a handful to your nose and inhale.

5. In the forest: Lie down and look up at all the giant trees and the sky beyond. Feel your back on the earth and let your eyes explore the canopy above. Find a tree and rub your back against it like a bear. Lean against the tree and stretch and arch your body. See if you can find a tree to hide behind and imagine you're an animal waiting to see who wanders by. Let yourself listen to the sound of leaves brushing against one another in the wind.

6. Anywhere: Make time to watch the sunset. You only get a finite number of sunsets in your life, so try to enjoy the changing colors and light whenever you can. Enjoying it with someone you love makes it extra awesome. If you're a morning person, pause and welcome the sun each morning, too!

See if connecting to nature helps you relate to your body with more patience and love.

38

Eat Like a Goddess

Years ago I asked my yoga students, "How would you treat yourself differently if you believed you were divine?" One student told me with a laugh, "If I believed I was divine, I wouldn't eat standing up over the counter." I agree. If I believed I was divine, I wouldn't eat behind the wheel of my car.

Can you imagine Aphrodite slurping down a veggie sandwich leaning over the kitchen counter (it would totally mess up her hair, and her toga...do you know how much the dry cleaning bills are for those things?) or Athena chowing down on a *carnitas asada* burrito behind the wheel of her convertible PT Cruiser? Seriously, the burrito is less believable than the car.

How *would* a goddess eat? Definitely sitting down. Preferably with servants waving palm fronds, serving peeled grapes... sorry, got a little carried away. How about with a single flower in the center of the table, a lovely glass of water with lemon, a freshly prepared dish in front of her with a variety of seasonal colors, textures, and flavors? As she settles into her chair, she takes a moment to enjoy the beauty of the food. As her eyes take in the rich hues, she imagines the vegetables growing on farms, the sun shining on them, the rain moistening their roots, the nimble bees pollinating each flower, and the hands tending them. She opens her hands around the plate and offers a blessing, "May all those who offer me this meal be blessed. May this food nourish me. May my energy and life honor all beings."

Then she sighs and lingers over each bite she takes in, enjoying every aspect and sensation of eating. Yum.

At the end of her meal, perhaps in the company of other smiling goddesses (and gods), she leans back in her seat, feeling full and sated.

Why don't we eat like goddesses? We're busy. We're tired. We have little ones to feed and laundry to do. We don't feel entitled to sit down and genuinely enjoy a meal.

But really, could you eat like a goddess once a day? How about once a week? Plan a goddess lunch with a friend, or make yourself a goddess meal. When you're planning a meal or going out to eat, ask yourself, *What does my inner goddess want to eat?*

My inner goddess loves:

Eating outside, at a café patio or in my own garden

A carafe of water at the table (especially mint and cucumber water)

Sweet red peppers (probably because they're seasonal and pricey!)

Figs and berries

Leafy salads with green goddess dressing (c'mon, what did you expect?)

Curried vegetables with daal, rice, and sauteed greens

Asparagus, avocado, and artichokes

Flowers—even in the food

Anything prepared with love and creativity

My inner goddess also likes to eat slowly and in the company of good friends (even if they're flowers). Listen to your inner goddess and let her teach you how to eat with great mindfulness and enjoyment. To nourish her, ask her what she needs, what she loves, and feed it to her. Slowly and with great love.

What does your inner goddess love?

39

Divine Body Salutation

Let this gentle movement help you slough off negativity and invite positive energy into your body. I find this sequence is a wonderful everyday practice that reminds my body it is whole, beautiful, and worthy of loving touch, whatever else is going on in my life.

1. Stand with your feet a comfortable distance apart. Feel your breath for a moment, how your chest lifts with your inhale, and how your belly softens with each exhale.

2. As you inhale, raise your arms over your head and touch the palms together in "prayer" position.

3. Keep the hands like this as you bend the elbows and bring them to the crown of your head.

4. Open the palms and let the hands slide down the sides of the head, sides of the neck, sides of the chest and waist. Keep letting the hands move down the outside of the legs and across the tops of the feet (or shins if

that's where you can reach), then back up the inside of the legs and up to the belly.

5. At the belly, cross the hands over each other and move them up the wrists, forearms, elbows, upper arms, and shoulders, then stroke the hands back down the arms to the belly once again.

6. Use your hands to rub and lightly massage your belly and your back from front to back at least three times.

7. Let your hands rest over your belly; close your eyes and notice how the movement and touch feels in your body. Is your body warmer? More energetic or calm? Happy? Just observe for a moment, then go through the entire sequence at least two more times, checking in each time at the end.

Once you're familiar with the sequence, give extra meaning to each round: on the first round, repeat to yourself, "I release from my body all negative thoughts and feelings from my day"; on the second, repeat, "I invite all good things into my body and experience"; on the third, "May I see and celebrate the beauty in this body and all bodies everywhere."

For a demonstration, I invite you to view a video of the Divine Body Salutation at http://www.kimberyoga.com/52 -ways-to-love-your-body/divine-body-salutation-video/.

40

Tackle an Impossible Task

I could never do a handstand as a kid. I remember watching my sister and her friends kick their legs up over their heads and hover against the yew bushes in the side yard—I wanted to join in but was terrified of flailing backwards through the air and landing in the shrubs, subjected to the shame of untangling myself from the branches while the older girls laughed. For this reason I was not a member of the exclusive Handstand Club, and my mind made it my body's fault that they ran off to play without me and my wobbly extremities. As an adult, when I found myself on a yoga mat, I hadn't realized handstands would be on the menu, and from the first time the teacher asked us to bring our mats up against the wall, the old terror returned.

But this time was different. Thanks to yoga, my arms were strong from practicing sweaty plank poses, and I had a growing sense of where my legs were in relation to the rest of my body even when I couldn't see them: to my surprise and relief, they didn't just disappear when out of view. As I crouched next to the wall, feeling the old fears gather for a reunion I was sure to be excluded from, the teacher stood beside me and spoke encouraging words into my ear, even holding my hips and helping me miraculously swing my legs up over my straightened, shaky arms. And suddenly there I was, in handstand. It was exhilarating.

It took years before I could kick up into handstand reliably on my own, but my body relished conquering something that represented my fear that maybe it wasn't just my inability to stand on my hands that made the other girls run away from me, but that they saw my secret unworthiness. I know now that my worthiness isn't dependent on my ability to do handstand. But handstand is an awesome thing my body can do now, and one way my body and I have triumphant fun together.

What's your handstand? What's the thing you thought your body would never be able to do? A friend of mine decided at nearly seventy years old to go back to ballet. She'd been told as a still-growing, ballet-obsessed child that she was too ungainly, tall, and big-footed to ever learn how to dance properly, and she quit. But she and her body never stopped wanting to dance. A sixty-year intermission was long enough, and she no longer cared whether anyone else thought she could dance "properly" or not. She discovered a beginner ballet class for adults and found herself relevé-ing and plié-ing at the barre with a permanent smile playing across her face.

What have you been told that you and your body could never do? Maybe it's running, or skydiving, or yoga. What childhood activity have you and your body always wanted to circle back to? See if you can find a qualified and patient instructor to teach you. Take it slow and easy, and let your body guide you one step at a time. Let trust grow and develop between you and your body. And remind yourself of your worthiness no matter what.

41

Dear Body, a Love Letter

Have you ever written a letter to your body? No? Why not? Tell your body how you feel about it. Be honest, be authentic. Share your disappointments, fears, longings, and dreams. Snuggle up and write your best-friend body a love letter. Here's mine:

Dear Body,

It's taken me a long time to get up the nerve to write you this letter. You deserve so much more than just a few pixels typed out on the computer. Think of this letter as warm socks, a shower of rose petals, and an afternoon playing in the surf all rolled up into one. It's a love letter of sorts…though it begins with an apology.

You've been incredibly dependable my whole life, taking care of me, hiking with me through the forest, dancing and making music, helping me expand into life in every possible way. And what did I do? I was mad at you for longer than I care to admit. I hid you out of shame. I made fun of you in front of other people. I starved you and mistreated you. I overfed you and then blamed you for existing. I invested time, energy, and money in developing my brain (an oversight you tolerated for years without complaint) and then resented you when you rebelled with pain. My humblest apologies don't nearly begin to touch the depth of what I put you through. I would never treat anyone else the way I've treated you. I'm so sorry.

I'm often disappointed when an apology doesn't include the oh-so-important corollary: "I'll make sure it never happens again." So…from now on I promise to do my very best to treat you with the love and respect you deserve. I might make mistakes, I might not love you perfectly at every moment, but know that I've resolved that nothing will stand in the way of me loving you ever again. No one's opinion, no bad mirrors, no ugly photos, no insults or hurt feelings: nothing will convince me that you aren't worth loving just the way you are.

You have been a best friend to me all this time, giving unconditional support to everything I love and create. *I want to do the same for you.* I want to listen to you and nurture you, see the beauty in you and support all the changes and adventures you have yet to experience. I want to be your best friend.

Teach me how to love you. Teach me how to listen. Remind me that your beauty is incomparable and inherent in what you are, a magnificent human body. Here are just a few things to remind us both of what I love about you:

You are strong, flexible, amazingly responsive, and adventurous.

Your hands reflect back to me my mother, my grandmother, and beyond even that…through you I see a long line of women's hands that have raised families, learned, loved, and shaped the world.

You are tall, yet steady. Solid, yet graceful. You are soft, but firm.

You are easily delighted: by rain on your face, by the softness of an animal's fur, by the rustle of leaves, by the sparkle of sunlight.

You are quiet and secretly wild. Other times you are loud and secretly in awe.

I love you. Thank you for being you. Thank you for loving me despite everything. I'm here for you. We're in this together. May I learn how to love you better every day.

Yours truly,

Kimber

42

Sacred Body

What is sacred to you? Notre Dame's massive stained glass windows arise first in my mind, and then an outdoor cathedral formed by enormous trees sheltering the forest floor. The first moment I held my baby son in my arms felt deeply sacred. In fact, the occasional hug in which my ear is placed near his chest and I hear his heart's steady beat still fills me with relief and quiet wonder.

What does sacred mean? To me it's whatever fills you with a sense of awe, effortlessly drawing your attention so that you can't help but pause, take it in, and hold for a reverent moment the tender and miraculous life we share.

We call certain places sacred—a temple, a holy marker, a cemetery, a river—and approach them with respect and dignity. Years ago I visited one of the gorgeous Buddhist monuments in Kathmandu,[25] and when I arrived at the base of the hill and looked up toward the dome at the top, I immediately felt drawn to its powerful energy. Once I'd climbed every stair and stood looking into the golden eyes of Buddha against the blue sky and watched the pilgrims circling the base, spinning the prayer wheels and murmuring their mantras, my heart wavered and expanded, filling my eyes with tears. Sacred. Any place that thousands, perhaps even millions, of people approach as sacred gathers palpable energy that can resonate in your body and soul whether or not you believe in the god-spirit honored there.

But we don't have to travel far to find something sacred. Some of us arrange objects sacred to our lives in our home to help focus our attention on what's important to us. When we treat the space with reverence, the objects themselves and even the coffee table altar they live on become sacred. We get a little peeved if an oblivious friend abandons a crumpled cup or gum wrapper there. If the forest or the beach feels like sacred space to you, leaving broken plastic wine glasses and crumpled paper napkins from your picnic to blow around in the grass and rocks feels sacrilegious. You wouldn't dream of it.

Why do we treat our bodies like they are less worthy than a temple or a forest? Is your body any less a miracle than the beach? Your human body is a work of evolutionary art, vastly more amazing in its complexity and mystery than the most elaborately constructed Gothic cathedral.

You've heard the phrase, "Your body is a temple." So—how is your temple? Do you treat your temple like sacred space? Or do you disrespect it? You wouldn't dream of breaking into someone's church or synagogue or mosque and spraying graffiti on the walls. Insulting, shaming, and abusing our bodies is like vandalizing our own church—using the altar cloths to wipe our feet, getting piss-drunk on the holy wine, and melting down the sacred objects to buy more spray paint. Here's a radical shift: instead, teach yourself to be the priestess of your sacred body.

Six steps to treat your body like a temple:

1. Recognize its beauty. See how extraordinary your body truly is. Look for what is good and right about it.

2. Approach your body with respect and awe. "Oh Nobly Born" (as the Buddha says), be gentle with and dignified toward your body. Offer your body loving rituals of cleansing.

3. Treat your body the way you would any other sacred space. Don't throw mental, emotional, and psychological "garbage" on it. Be kind and responsible.

4. Honor it. Listen to what food, movement, rest, and attention it needs and meet those needs appropriately. Dress your body with attention to the comfort and ease that allows its beauty to shine fully.

5. Protect it. Avoid people who don't treat your body with the respect it deserves and situations that endanger its well-being.

6. Pause and enjoy it. Experience and appreciate your own aliveness. Slow down and savor your life.

Your body is sacred space. Meet it with reverence and delight. Be the temple.

43

Take Small Steps, Daily Practice

If you want to love your body, you can't just do nice things for your body every once in a while.

Think of it like brushing your teeth. How would it feel if you only brushed your teeth once a week? Once a month? No way. All that yellow fuzzy stuff and bits of food just sitting there…need I go on?

When I don't take the time to love my body every day, a creeping sense of dissatisfaction crawls under my skin, and the old tapes of self-criticism and negativity play in the background like the noise of a street party through an open window.

Unless you live in an off-grid yurt, you get bombarded from the moment you wake up in the morning until your eyes close at night with the message that you're not fit enough, not attractive enough, not enough enough. Until I figured out how to manage ads in my email, every time I opened my inbox, I'd get some side bar advertisement inviting me to join Jenny Craig or promising the secret to lose belly fat. I finally lost it when a Special K ad popped up challenging me to lose ten pounds in ten days. *Hey, I need those ten pounds! You can't have them!*

Think of loving your body every day as preventative. It cleans out the junk, the nonessentials, the judgments, and leaves you with a healthy, clean feeling that nine out of ten dentists recommend. Okay, just kidding about that last part.

Here's the love your body equivalent of brushing your teeth in the morning, the Good Morning Body:

1. As you wake up, let yourself stretch like a cat. Before you even get out of bed, reach your arms up, stretch your legs out, and wiggle your toes.

2. Curl up into a ball for a moment and thank your body for everything it did during the night, letting your mind rest and reset, digesting, relaxing, healing.

3. Relax back into the bed for a moment and gently touch your feet and legs; touch your belly and hips; touch your shoulders, arms, and chest; touch your neck and face and head. As you touch your body, say "Good morning" to each part in turn.

4. To finish, bring one hand to your belly and one hand to your heart, and make a love your body aspiration for today: "May I be kind to you today. May we have a great day together. May I treat you as a friend."

Then, slowly sit up and enjoy the rest of your day!

You can print out these four steps and set them on your bedside table as a reminder to do them as you get up in the morning. Try it every day for a week and see how it goes...may you find more love toward your body with each sunrise.

44

Rest and Revitalize

Give yourself an instant spa day by inviting your body into a restorative yoga pose, where you can rest, breathe, and relax. A friend of mind calls it "sleepy yoga." I love doing sleepy yoga on a wide couch, on the bed, or on the floor. Gather some pillows from the rest of the house and build yourself a cozy place to enjoy these poses.

1. Reclining Goddess Pose

   Great name, isn't it? It's easy to feel like a goddess when you've built a comfy nest to rest in. Find a place on the floor or bed. Sit down and put the soles of your feet together, widening the knees apart. Put a pillow behind your back, right up against your hips. Put another couple of pillows under your knees to support them. Then lie back onto the pillow behind you. Feel free to add another pillow under your head to get really comfortable and relaxed. You may also want to place a blanket over your body or even a fragrant eye pillow over your eyes.

Lie here and breathe. Set a timer if you like, but give yourself anywhere from five to twenty minutes to just relax and enjoy. If at any time your body starts to feel uncomfortable, feel free to move into another pose.

2. Legs up the Wall Pose

Though it's called "legs up the wall" pose, you can do it on a chair or couch, too—anyplace it's comfortable for your back to be straight on the floor and your legs elevated. The idea is simply to lie on your back with your legs supported against a wall, or bent over a chair or couch.

Have a small pillow handy to use under your head, and maybe another for under your hips or legs. Lie on the floor on your side with your hips and feet close to the wall, chair, or couch. Bend your knees in toward your chest, and scoot yourself up close so that your hips and butt are up against the wall, legs of the chair, or edge of the couch. Then turn onto your back, and position your body so that you are perpendicular to the wall (or the back of the chair or couch). Swing your legs either straight up against the wall or onto the seat. Bring the pillow under your head and place another under your lower back if you're against the wall, or under your legs if you're using a piece of furniture. One friend of mine does this in her bed at night, her legs up against the headboard, and finds it helps her fall back to sleep.

Lie here and breathe for five to twenty minutes. Feel your chest lift with the inhale and soften on the exhale. You can do some loving-kindness practice here (see chapter 7) or think about what you're grateful for in your body and your life.

To exit the pose, bend your knees up into your chest, roll over onto your side, and use your arms to push yourself back up to sitting on the floor.

3. Supported Nap Pose

This is one of my favorites, and it's so simple to do in the middle of the day if you have a chance to lie down and nap or just relax for a few minutes. It's especially helpful when you've been asking a lot of your body. It's good to have at least one pillow for under the knees and possibly a second one for under the head. Sit on the floor or bed with your legs in front of you and bring a pillow under your slightly bent knees. Lie down on your back, and place a pillow under your head if that's comfortable. Let each inhale help you notice without judgment where there is tension or tightness in the body, and let each exhale be an invitation for the body to relax and release that tension. Breathe in a sense of compassion for yourself and your body and breathe out compassion for all bodies everywhere. Rest here for five to twenty minutes, then bring that sense of stillness and ease into the rest of your day.

45

Never Give Up, Never Surrender

Don't tell me. You've tried being friendlier to your body, you've tried seeing the good in it, you've tried imagining it as a magnificent pillar of evolutionary achievement, but you're still not feeling the love. Don't worry. There's still time. As long as you're alive, as long as you have a body, there's always time to fall in love with it.

If you're feeling discouraged, don't panic. Many of us have a lifetime of negativity toward our bodies that takes more than a day, a week—or, dare I say, forty-five chapters—to undo.

Perhaps you looked in the mirror this morning and saw your mean girl sneering back at you, or found yourself machine-eating your way through a box of Girl Scout cookies instead of taking care of yourself. That's okay. Give yourself a break.

What would your best friend say? Again, we're talking about your idealized best friend, not meanies like Simon Cowell or Ann Coulter. Your best friend who sees the best in you, who knows your faults and flaws, and loves you because of the complicated person you are, not in spite of it. Your best friend knows your secret talents and amazing skills, has watched you live through broken bones and new-love jitters, and supports you unconditionally. She also doesn't put up with more than a minute or two of self-pity and rationalizing.

Your best friend would say, "Oh honey, let it go. One step back doesn't undo your two steps forward, and even if it did, you're still on the right track. Keep moving. You've tackled harder stuff than this. We're in this together."

"We're in this together" are magic words for me. I whisper those words to my body and imagine my body whispering them back. In those moments when I'm feeling anxious about some new challenge life has thrown at me, "Body, you and I, we're in this together" is exactly what calms my blood pressure and fortifies my inner confidence.

Look back at the exercises and practices for learning to love your body that we've covered so far: say "Hi" to your reflection; let go of old, yucky rules about our bodies and replace them with new ones; imagine meeting and conversing with your inner best friend and your inner demon; set aspirations for how you want to feel about your body; dialogue with the body about past trauma; make a list of things you like about your body; and so on. Which have you tried? Which have resonated most with you?

When my inner critic starts going off about how she's sure my pajamas didn't fit this tightly last week, instead of worrying that she's about to implement her plans for world domination, I take it as an early warning system alert. Did I get enough sleep?

Have I been eating well? Did my body get movement it enjoys today? Have I been forgetting my morning self-massage? Did I have a sucky day, and my heart needs soothing? I like to think of my inner critic as unskillfully speaking up for what my body needs, like a dog who barks when she really just wants her ears scratched.

Four of the most important words I ever heard came from one of my first yoga teachers: "Be patient with yourself." Be patient, keep coming back to the practices in this book, find others that work for you, and discard the practices that don't. Fall over, trip, backslide, lie there for a while and decide you just can't do it, and then get up just one more time.

46

Expect Change

S ure, maybe I can learn to love my body today, but what about tomorrow's body? Or next year's? Or next decade's? I'm not a psychic and can't look into the smoky crystal ball to see into your future, but there is one thing I can absolutely guarantee: your body is going to change. It's going to get sick and injured and it's going to have pain. It's going to gain weight and lose weight. It's going to get crow's-feet and smile lines and cellulite and stretch marks in places you didn't know it was possible. Your body's going to sag, no matter how many crunches you do or how many times you—heaven help us—put yourself under the knife. And if you're lucky, if you live long enough, even your wrinkles will have wrinkles.

There you go, I said it—the truth we don't like to think about or admit, but that's always in the back of our minds. Your body is going to age. You are aging right now, as you read these words. Expect change, embrace change, and your relationship with your body will grow and deepen in the most unexpected ways.

We resist change in our bodies. Some of us even unconsciously try to make deals with our bodies that we know are impossible to live up to: "I'll love you so long as you fit into my favorite dress." Or, "Body, you and I are best friends as long as we still get carded at the store." This is conditional love—love that depends on some outer condition for our affection to continue. And if that condition—no matter how outrageous—isn't met, we feel entitled to turn our metaphorical back on our body and leave it in the corner with its dunce cap on.

In the messy midst of learning to love my body, I looked into the mirror one morning with a sigh and said, "Maybe I can love my body right now, today, just the way it is, but no promises about tomorrow." Seriously, what if my body went berserk and started growing hair between my fingers, sprouted wings or horns, or, god forbid, gained weight? Then all bets would be off. But as I looked again in the mirror at the same body that had been through infancy, puberty, and pregnancy with me, how could I imagine that it wasn't going to change? (Although wings are admittedly unlikely.)

But whatever changes my body goes through, I want to support it and give it the best care and attention I can. After all, we're in this together. What's the point of loving some snapshot of my body, when what I really want is to love my body through thick and thin, 'til death do we part?

Why not open up to a more loving attitude toward ourselves: one of unconditional love? A love that embraces change and does not depend on a particular reflection in the mirror, a specific number on the scale, or even the ability to walk or elicit compliments from others.

Visualize a relationship with your body that supports all the changes it has been through and will go through. What would it feel like to have that relationship? What would it mean to you to have a durable friendship with your body through all the good times and the bad?

47

Try Something New

Bodies enjoy routine, knowing that they are going to get the food, rest, and activity they need every day. Bodies also like to be surprised sometimes…to have a new experience, to try something they've never tried before, and feel something they've never felt before.

Recently I had my first mud bath. It had been a while since I'd given my body something fun and new to experience, and I figured it was love your body research. Field trip! I told my body, "Look, I have no idea what this is going to be like, and if you really hate it, we can leave." In the description of the mud bath, I noticed words that make my body perk up and get excited the same way my dog does when you say the words *walk* or *park*— *mineral bath, steam room, blanket-wrapped, cucumbers on your eyelids*—so I figured there were parts my body would enjoy for sure. We would see how it goes, just like going off on an adventure with a friend to a new place neither one of you is sure you'll like, but seems intriguing.

And when I was lying there, with mud packed all over my naked body, my body had a moment of "What the hell is this?"

And so I lay there and reassured my body that we were okay, that it was just for fifteen minutes, that we could get out at any time. I let my mind and body explore together all the new sensations: the feeling of warm, heavy volcanic mud on my chest and belly; the sense that the mud was hotter underneath my back and legs than on top; the grainy smoothness of the mud as my fingers rubbed it between them; even the occasional desire to jump out, mud flying everywhere, and hose off immediately. At one point, the woman who was guiding me through the process offered me a cool towel for my forehead. I said no thanks, but a few moments later, as sweat erupted on my forehead, my body was like, "Uh, if we're not getting out yet, we're gonna need that cold towel. Ask for it." And I did.

My body thought the whole mud bath thing was interesting, though it was less than thrilled about having to dig mud out of all its private creases in the shower afterward while other people milled about the room. It did love lying in the private mineral bath, the glass of cucumber and orange water that was continually offered and refilled, and the blanket-wrapped nap with cucumber-soothed eyelids at the end. I'm not sure I'll go again, but it was awesome to do something that was entirely about letting my skin experience something brand new: hot mud.

What has your body always wanted to try? What would be something fun, some new sensation or experience?

1. Pick a new experience and check in with your body about its level of interest. A yoga class? A surfing lesson? A zip-lining trip? A cold plunge? A hot-stone massage? Listen for your body's message: a little tilt of the head, a metaphorical wagging of the tail, whatever signal your body gives to tell you, "That sounds like fun."

2. Schedule it. Put it in your calendar and show up. Also, remind and reassure your body that you don't have to go through with it, that you can leave anytime, and that it's intended to be a fun adventure together, not an attempt to overwhelm the body or push it to an extreme it won't enjoy.

3. Go on your adventure and keep tuning into the body over and over, asking it how it's doing, comforting it, reminding it you're on the same team and taking care of each other. Have as much fun as you can, and check in with your body later about how it went. Reflect on what parts you liked and didn't like, and whether you'd do it again.

4. Give your body lots of positive feedback and gratitude: "I really appreciated it when you told me *this*. Wasn't *that* part fun? Thanks for trying out a new adventure with me!"

48

Every Body Needs a Friend

Walking down the street, I used to have two different reactions to women's bodies. The first was disgust tempered with pity...*Ew, I would never want to look like that, poor thing.* The second was jealousy...*OMG how does she do it? I wish I looked like that! Ugh, so unfair!*

I was caught between aversion and attraction—rejecting what I didn't want and resenting what I didn't have but wanted. You can imagine that by grouping every woman into the category of "I'm sorry for you" or "I hate you," I wasn't going to gain any fans. Casting oneself as the Great Uber Judge of All Bodies is a lonely role to play.

Weirdly, I did not wear my Uber Judge hat with my friends. They were wonderful. I loved them: their looks were not the point. Susan's eyes warmed me, Tab looked adorable in braids, and Deidre's light-up dimples could eradicate my worst moods. But the minute I found myself surrounded by a group of strangers, I'd pull my safe, lofty, body-judge hat over my ears and eyes and let the judgments fall where they may. And when I wore that Uber Judge hat, I assumed all those around me were wearing their Uber Judge hats as well, throwing their own judgments my way, thereby making every trip to the store a running gauntlet of self-consciousness, resentment, and pity.

Fortunately, at some point I realized that my internal ranking system was a little, shall we say, superficial? All my body judgments served no purpose but to make me exhausted and crazy. If I could appreciate the sparkle in Susan's eyes and not worry about her dress size, couldn't I do the same thing with the woman walking down the street toward me? Could I enjoy someone wearing a lovely dress without wishing I was her, and hating being me?

I didn't know it at the time, but there's a Buddhist concept that neatly encapsulates the idea of being joyful for someone else's success. It's called *mudita*, or sympathetic joy.

Could I look for beauty everywhere, and be happy for its existence? Imagine the freedom of walking down the street and instead of feeling frustrated and hateful, feeling light, open, and joyful. Instead of every person increasing your desire to cower in the shadows, every person you see could increase your happiness.

There are three basic steps for this:

1. See something good in each person you see. (This might take some practice.)

2. Be glad for them. (Think of them as someone you genuinely want to be happy.)

3. At the same time, appreciate what is good about you (not seeing yourself as better or worse than anyone else, but recognizing your own uniqueness).

You can practice with a list of people in your life you want to feel sympathetic joy for. Go through the first two steps above for each person, and check in with yourself periodically with the third step, remembering to see what is good about you. If you still find yourself feeling envious of someone on your list, ask yourself, *What is it about this person's life that I want for myself? How can I invite that quality or experience into my life?* If you still find yourself feeling pity for someone on the list, ask yourself, *What is it about this person's life that I avoid or fear? Can I soften around that fear and acknowledge that I have the resourcefulness and resilience to meet whatever life offers me?* Invite a genuine feeling of well-wishing into your heart for all of these people, seeing their goodness and feeling joy for them. You may find this practice like taking a bath in love: wonderfully refreshing and transformative.

When I let go of being the Great Uber Judge of All Bodies, I finally saw all the beauty I'd been missing…in myself and others.

49

Trust Yourself

Your body is a certifiable genius. It can do things even the most brilliant minds on the planet can't recreate. It knows how to pick up a grape without crushing it. It hears and sees and moves. It senses invisible scents from far away and draws from your memory where you've smelled them before. It laughs and shakes, all the while keeping its parts in their designated places. It's a multitasking champion: digesting, healing, breathing, thinking, and protecting you from inner and outer dangers even while you're asleep. Your body knows so much about you. It knows what's good.

But instead of trusting and listening to our bodies, we're taught to believe that experts know more than we do. Don't get me wrong, I love experts and studies. The problem is when we trust an expert to know what is best for us without ever checking in with our bodies. Dieting is a perfect example of this. We absorb an outside expert's idea about what our body should weigh, and then try to eat and exercise in the prescribed way without ever taking into consideration how our body feels. In fact, we often use expert advice as an excuse for completely ignoring the body's needs for rest and food. We end up looking in the mirror and judging ourselves, feeling detached and critical of the body, whether or not the diet "works."

So listen to the experts. Read the studies. And know that their opinions and findings may or may not apply to you and your body. Don't give responsibility for taking care of your body to someone else. Try out any advice that sounds compelling to you by asking your body if it sounds like a good idea first. Then take some small steps in that direction, and keep checking in with your body all along the way. In my experience, my body enjoys being nudged, not pushed. It likes it when it has the chance to feel how some new change settles. My body appreciates slow, incremental change that respects its animal nature and its autonomy. It likes to feel respected and loved no matter what.

Say you want to eat more vegetables. Experts agree, studies show that eating more vegetables is good for you and your body. It seems like a great idea, so what could go wrong? You make the decision to pile your plate full of kale and spinach and green beans without asking your body if it likes any of those things. You force yourself to eat tons of brussels sprouts, which you could never stand as a kid, and purple cabbage, which you always thought was an inedible decorative plant. You go on like this for a week, eating as many vegetables and salads as you can manage, until you can't bear to chew on another raw carrot. It may be months before you can stomach another salad, and then you remember, *Oh yeah, I tried eating more veggies but it didn't work out.* You decide maybe you just don't like vegetables.

Here's a different way to approach the same effort: Ask your body if it would like to try eating more vegetables. Ask it what vegetables it likes. Give it plenty of the vegetables it loves, and notice how it feels afterward. Invite it to try small bites of the vegetables it doesn't care for, and see how it feels afterward. (They say sometimes we have to taste something more than twenty times before our taste buds start to enjoy it.) Experiment with vegetables you've never had before: kohlrabi, kabucha squash, mizuna greens. Just try and see. Reassure your body, "Anything you hate, we don't have to eat." Keep listening to your body, keep feeding it vegetables it loves, and keep exploring to see what new flavors and recipes help widen its selection and enjoyment.

When you listen and treat your body with respect, you not only create a new habit around eating—you also create a base level of trust and connection with this body you inhabit, this body that is your life.

When do you trust your body most? What activities connect you to the wisdom of your body? What keeps you from trusting and listening to your body? When you're having a hard time making a decision, try pausing and asking your body what you should do. Your body has shared every birthday with you, has learned every activity you've ever learned, has been through every trauma and triumph with you. It's a big, wise, grounded being that always wants what's best for you. It's always with you. Dig deep and mine its wisdom.

50

Love Your Body Manifesto

I wrote this manifesto to remind all of us on this love your body journey about the big picture. Read through it, add your own points, or even write your own manifesto. If this manifesto really resonates with you and you want a copy to hang someplace you can see it everyday, feel free to download it as a beautiful original poster from my website at http://www.kimberyoga.com/52-ways-to-love-your-body/love-your-body-manifesto/.

1. We recognize that our bodies are flooded with messages from media, family, peers, strangers, and ourselves about how we should look.

2. We acknowledge that body image is not fixed: we can change how we feel about our bodies by changing how we think and act.

3. No one right way exists to "love your body"; there are only tools that work for us and tools that don't.

4. Loving our bodies doesn't happen overnight. It requires persistence, kindness, and patience.

5. We expect setbacks as we learn to love our bodies. We do not expect our relationship with our bodies to be perfect or always easy.

6. Loving our bodies requires going to a dark place sometimes, unearthing our judgments, fears, and vulnerabilities.

7. We know that the rewards of learning to love our bodies are vast, including less self-judgment, more energy for the things we love, and better relationships with others.

8. Community support is vital to loving our bodies; therefore, we show respect for other bodies by withholding judgments and comparisons.

9. We reject pressure to find the right diet, lose (or gain) weight, or exercise to develop an ideal body. We embrace supporting our physical and emotional well-being, listening to and trusting the body's wisdom, and learning to relate to the body with kindness through all the changes it goes through in life. We create healthy boundaries against body negativity and invite in positive experiences that support body love.

10. As we grow in love for ourselves, we move society as a whole in the direction of acceptance and seeing the worthiness of all bodies everywhere.

51

Loving Your Body Is Not Just About You

For some of us, "using our power for good and not for evil" (to quote the kindly adult mentor of junior superheroes everywhere) is motivation enough to learn how to relate to our bodies in a more healthy way. We recognize how we've been misusing our energy to hurt ourselves and are ready to channel that energy into supporting our dreams instead of tearing ourselves down. For others, we need to connect our journey to the big picture...it's not enough to do it for ourselves. We want to feel like our efforts around loving our bodies are going to make the world a better place, not mire us in navel-gazing and self-indulgence. Remember Emily, the little girl who said, "My body is my best friend"? I have four words for you: "Do it for her."

Imagine this six-year-old girl with perfect confidence and joy in her body just as she is. How long do you think that's going to last? Until her first injury, a broken wrist or sprained ankle? Until the first middle school mean girl comment—"You're fat"? Until her first period, or when her hips grow and her breasts start showing? Until she starts to internalize the billboards and magazine covers and starts thinking she should look like an airbrushed model? You can see it coming, like a storm approaching over the horizon, with few places to huddle in safety, and no sense of when it might pass. Emily hears her friends talking about whatever the latest fad diet is. She tries it, but gains weight instead. In college, she joins her friends in criticizing their bodies at the gym and forgets she ever loved her body like a best friend. In a handful of years, a dozen at most, she's experiencing the same agony, the same disgust, the same frustration and alienation from her body that so many of us suffered through.

Now imagine that same girl, same circumstances. Except that her mom, her teachers at school, her karate instructor, her doctor, the chatty woman at the salon who cuts her hair, her teenage babysitter, even the women she sees walking down the street, clearly love their bodies, feel confident in whatever size they are, never compare themselves to other women, and encourage her to treat her body with the dignity, respect, and friendliness it deserves.

Do you see?

Every woman who transforms her own relationship with her body from one of struggle to one of ease makes it easier for Emily to love her body for her entire life. Each woman who does this inner work helps shift the culture as a whole, from one where our bodies are battlegrounds to one where our bodies are the source of inspiration and support for everything we create in life.

Your transformation matters. Your ability to shift how you feel about your body can change the world.

Think about it. When you criticize your body, who hears your critique? Your friends? Your partner? How do they feel when they hear you say, "My body is so ugly"? One woman's boyfriend explained, "When you say that about your body, it makes me feel like there's something wrong with me for loving you." When a group of friends gets together, if one person starts to criticize her hips, another goes off about her thighs, and the next about her belly, suddenly everyone feels the need to prove she has the most disgusting body that ever walked on two feet. Does anyone ever feel good about oneself after a competitive body-bashing conversation?

The good news is that the opposite happens as well. When you love your body, when you treat your body with friendliness, when you say respectful and loving things about your body, people hear you. Your confidence and sense of being at home in your body puts others at ease and turns you into a wonderful role model for self-care. Treating your own body with friendliness gives others permission to relate to their own with more respect and kindness. Together we can make sure that Emily grows up in a world surrounded by women who live the truth that all bodies are worthy of love.

In the final chapter, I'll share with you some more ways to support the Emilys you know and love.

Teach Your Children
[to Love Their Bodies] Well

D o you have an "Emily" in your home, or in your life? Do you teach her to treat her body like a scapegoat, or like a treasured friend?

Kids can teach us a lot about loving our bodies…how to cannonball into a lake, jump for joy, and spin until we fall over. How to have fun in our bodies for the grass-stained, muddy-kneed delight of it.

Most kids are already experts at how to enjoy and love their kid bodies. What they learn from *us* is how adults relate to their bodies. Here are the top five rules kids learn about bodies from the adults in their lives:

1. Never compliment your own body. In fact, put your body down every time you look at it. Never miss an opportunity to criticize your body in front of other people.

2. If an item of clothing looks bad on you, it's your body's fault. If you're in a bad mood, it's probably your body's

fault, too. If you didn't get a date last week, or the job you wanted—it's your body's fault. Any time you're pissed off about anything, it's probably because your body is sabotaging you.

3. It's okay to make fun of fat people, because it's not okay to be fat.

4. It's fine to talk about how your friend needs to go on a diet behind her back, or even to her face.

5. Exercise should be difficult, painful, and hard to force yourself to do. You should force yourself to do it anyway, and feel bad about yourself if you don't.

Yikes. These are cringe-worthy, and you could swear you've never demonstrated any of them in front of a child. But you know how kids are; they're sponges. They soak up every comment muttered under your breath in front of a mirror, every overheard conversation about someone's "weight problem," every time we smile and nod at a fat joke. Kids are natural imitators. Every gesture, movement, and facial expression you make in their presence gets filed away in their brains under the heading "This Is How Adults Act." And you know damn well they'll try out everything in that file at least once on their way to figuring out what kind of adult they're going to be. You don't even have to write these rules up and post them on the fridge:

almost every girl knows these rules by heart by the time she's twelve (if not much earlier), and every boy by at least fourteen.

The good news is you can change the rules.

Here's what you do:

1. Compliment yourself out loud in front of the mirror every day. Some days your kid will overhear you and think you're nuts. But slowly the message will sink in… it's okay to appreciate your body.

2. Compliment your children's bodies, physical ability, and appearance (feel free to include their intelligence, sense of humor, and persistence, too!). "Your hair looks great today." "Your handstand is amazing." "Your body is so strong!" By seeing what's good in them we help insulate them from both bullies and flatterers.

3. Never, ever, ever criticize your body in front of anyone else, especially your child. In fact, get out of the habit of criticizing your body, even in your own head. Your body is not a scapegoat for whatever is wrong today. If a swimsuit looks crappy on you, it's the swimsuit's fault…not your body's. Address the true pain and discomfort of what you're feeling instead of blaming it on your weight or size.

4. Don't make fat jokes. Don't laugh at fat jokes. You probably don't tell racist or homophobic jokes and you

sure don't teach your kids to laugh at them. Being fat is a natural part of human diversity. Read nutritionist Linda Bacon's book, *Health At Every Size,* to understand the function and myths about fat in our lives.[26]

5. Respect other people's bodies. Don't make weight and dieting a topic of conversation. Aren't there more important things to talk about? World peace? Organ donation? How to survive the impending zombie apocalypse? (By the way, it's fine to make fun of zombies.)

6. Have fun exercising! Let your child see you having fun exercising. Do exercise you love, and while it's fine to complain (a little) about aches and pains, emphasize how much you enjoy dancing the tango, swimming, skiing, hiking, skating, riding a unicycle, whatever your body loves to do.

7. You don't have to tell your child, "I love my body and you should love yours, too." Instead, live it! Let your whole life reflect the love and appreciation you have for your body, and your child will soak it up like a sponge in a bubble bath.

Live in your body the way you want your children to live in theirs. Treat your body with love and your child will learn… THIS is how adults treat their bodies.

Acknowledgments

Without the unconditional support of Chris Simpkins, this book would still be a mere idea in my head. Thank you, love. You make all things possible.

No words exist for how grateful I am to Catharine Meyers for seeing the beauty and necessity of this work. Thank you to Jess Beebe, Karen Hathaway, Julie Bennett, Cassie Kolias, Bridget Kinsella, Justin Demeter, freelance editor Rona Bernstein, and the whole amazing team at New Harbinger.

Hayley Ebersole and Kelly Rafferty, thank you for your own journeys in treating your bodies with more love and for your generous support of the work and the students.

Zubin Shroff, Saraswati Clere, Kimberly Leo, Mae Boscana, and the folks at Westerbeke Ranch, I am so grateful for how beautifully you have created spaces for students to find love for themselves through yoga.

For continued inspiration and for challenging me to take these practices deeper and wider, I thank Rick Hanson, Linda Graham, Brené Brown, Linda Bacon, Cheryl Strayed, Marilyn Wann, Ragen Chastain, and the wonderful folks who make up ASDAH (Association for Size Diversity and Health).

For bringing spirit and mindfulness to the practices, I thank Pema Chödrön, Sharon Salzberg, Ruth King, Kevin Griffin, Wes Nisker, and Shahara Godfrey.

Endless thanks to my dear friends who remind me over and over to keep going, have fun, and stay open: Nishanga Bliss, Andrea Scher, Mati McDonald, Stephanie Haffner, and Carolyn Brown.

For their inspiration, friendship, and contribution, I thank Signe Darpinian, Karen Scheuner, Rajen Thapa, Valerie Tookes, Kathleen Antonia, Marissa Baumann, Lana Simmons, and Kai Nicole.

Thank you to Laurie Wagner and the Wednesday morning writers for all the feedback and focus, and to Heather Monroe Pierce and the dancing tribe of women for keeping me in my body.

Thank you to Miryam Sas, Elizabeth Bogan, and Kenyatta Monroe-Sinkler. Our brilliant writing group was all your idea.

A final thanks to Rachel Medanic and Jean-Marie Moore for your enthusiasm and support; to Cooper and our whole extended family for putting up with my deadlines; to Spencer Smith and to Peter Ashbaugh and your team for all of the technical, web, and marketing work; and to all the Love Your Body students for everything you've taught me about how to share this work more authentically.

And to the all the readers of *Full*…thank you for letting my story fill your heart.

Notes

1 Kimber Simpkins, *Full: How I Learned to Satisfy My Insatiable Hunger and Feed My Soul* (Oakland, CA: New Harbinger Publications, 2015).

2 From Rainer Maria Rilke, "Go to the Limits of Your Longing," trans. Joanna Macy and Anita Barrows.

3 Rick Hanson, *Buddha's Brain* (Oakland, CA: New Harbinger Publications, 2009), 5–19.

4 Elizabeth Gilbert, *Eat, Pray, Love: One Woman's Search for Everything Across Italy, India and Indonesia* (New York: Penguin Books, 2006), 55.

5 Brené Brown, "The Power of Vulnerability," TedX Houston. June 2010. 6:34.

6 Roman Krznaric, *How Should We Live?* (Katonah, NY: Blue Bridge, 2013), 4–11.

7 David Carle, *Introduction to Air in California* (Berkeley, CA: University of California Press, 2006), xiii.

8   Anne Lamott, "My Mind Is a Bad Neighborhood I Try Not to Go into Alone," *Salon*, March 13, 1997, http://www.salon.com/1997/03/13/lamott970313/

9   Pema Chödrön, "Good Medicine," [audio CD], (Louisville, CO: Sounds True, March 1, 2001).

10 For more information on how to do formal loving-kindness practice, see Pema Chödrön's audio CD, "Good Medicine," and Sharon Salzberg's book, *Lovingkindness: The Revolutionary Art of Happiness* (Boston: Shambhala, 2002).

11 John Gottman, *Why Marriages Succeed or Fail* (New York: Simon & Schuster, 1994), 20.

12 Ibid., 56–61.

13 Shaun Dreisbach, "Shocking Body-Image News: 97% of Women Will Be Cruel to Their Bodies Today," *Glamour*, February 2011, http://www.glamour.com/health-fitness/2011/02/shocking-body-image-news-97-percent-of-women-will-be-cruel-to-their-bodies-today

14 Pema Chödrön, "How We Get Hooked and How We Get Unhooked." *Shambhala Sun*, March 1, 2003, http://www.lionsroar.com/how-we-get-hooked-shenpa-and-how-we-get-unhooked/

15 Ruth King, *Healing Rage: Women Making Inner Peace Possible* (New York: Penguin, 2008).

16 Jean Kilbourne, "Slim Hopes: Advertising & The Obsession With Thinness," *Media Education Foundation Study Guide*, 1994, http://www.mediaed.org/assets /products/305/studyguide_305.pdf

17 Margery Williams, *The Velveteen Rabbit Or How Toys Become Real* (New York: Macmillan, 1988), 7–8.

18 Nathaniel Hawthorne, "The Birth-Mark," *The Pioneer*, Vol. 1, Issue 3, March 1843.

19 Steven Furtick, "One reason we struggle w/ insecurity: we're comparing our behind the scenes to everyone else's highlight reel." Tweet, @stevenfurtick. May 10, 2011. The concept of comparing our insides to other people's outsides is a well-known part of the recovery and Alcoholics Anonymous community. "Never compare your insides to everyone else's outsides" is also sometimes attributed to Anne Lamott, a well-known member of the recovery community.

20 Tara Parker-Pope, "Go Easy on Yourself, a New Wave of Research Urges." *New York Times*, February 28, 2011, http://well.blogs.nytimes.com/2011/02/28/go-easy -on-yourself-a-new-wave-of-research-urges/

21 Linda Bacon, *Health at Every Size: The Surprising Truth About Your Weight* (Dallas, TX: Ben Bella Books, 2008), 125.

22 My quotation is a paraphrasing of the *sutta* referenced here, based on my understanding: Thanissaro Bhikkhu, trans. "Sallatha Sutta: The Arrow," SN 36.6, http://www.accesstoinsight.org/tipitaka/sn/sn36/sn36.006.than.html

23 Dr. Nishanga Bliss in discussion with the author, Jan 11, 2015.

24 Walt Whitman, *Leaves of Grass* (Boston: Small, Maynard & Company, 1904), 54.

25 Swayambhunath in Kathmandu has since been damaged by the tragic 2015 earthquake.

26 Linda Bacon, *Health at Every Size: The Surprising Truth About Your Weight* (Dallas, TX: Ben Bella Books, 2008).

Kimber Simpkins is a writer, body-image coach, Anusara-influenced yoga instructor, and author of *Full*. Her successful shift away from secret body hating to public body loving inspires her yoga students and readers everywhere. A former civil rights lawyer, Kimber has devoted the last seventeen years to the intensive study of yoga and meditation, and has been delighted by yoga's ability to bring joy to every aspect of life. She teaches weekly classes, Love Your Body workshops, and yoga retreats in Northern California and elsewhere. As a supporter of Health at Every Size (HAES) and the Yoga and Body Image Coalition (YBIC), Kimber welcomes students of all sizes and levels. You can find out more about Kimber at www.kimberyoga.com.

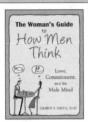

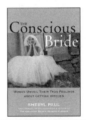